TRICOTER

Simply Beautiful

SWEATERS FOR MEN

Linden Phelps and Beryl Hiatt

Martingale™
& COMPANY

Simply Beautiful Sweaters for Men
© 2001 by Linden Phelps and Beryl Hiatt

Martingale & Company
20205 144th Ave. NE
Woodinville, WA 98072-8478
www.martingale-pub.com

CREDITS

President · Nancy J. Martin
CEO · Daniel J. Martin
Publisher · Jane Hamada
Editorial Director · Mary V. Green
Editorial Project Manager · Tina Cook
Technical Editor · Ursula Reikes
Copy Editor · Pamela Mostek
Design and Production Manager · Stan Green
Illustrator · Robin Strobel
Cover and Text Designer · Trina Stahl
Photographer · Brent Kane

Printed in Hong Kong
06 05 04 03 02 01   8 7 6 5 4 3 2 1

**Library of Congress
Cataloging-in-Publication Data**

Phelps, Linden.
  Simply beautiful sweaters for men / Linden
    Phelps and Beryl Hiatt.
    p.   cm.
    ISBN 1-56477-379-5
    1. Knitting—Patterns. 2. Sweaters. 3. Men's
clothing. I. Hiatt, Beryl. II. Title.

TT825.P45 2001
746.43'20432—dc21

                                        2001022222

MISSION STATEMENT

We are dedicated to providing quality products and service by working together to inspire creativity and to enrich the lives we touch.

Dedication

◆ ◆ ◆

We have been incredibly fortunate to have been surrounded, supported, and encouraged by a number of unique men, each of whom has enriched our lives and our knowledge. Each of these, whether friend, family, or lover, has become an integral fiber in the tapestry of our lives and has therefore played a significant role in the creation of this book.

As we considered the influences that brought us to this point, one man in particular stood out as a primary force. Stacy Charles has supported us professionally from our first introductions—even when that meant limiting our purchases (reducing his profits to ensure our long-term success), counseling us to go slowly, to consider our ability to sell through stock each season, and to avoid getting carried away by the moment.

It is Stacy who has given us the opportunity to test the newest and most exciting yarns each season, allowing us to devise new patterns that stretch our creativity. He has helped us develop a tradition of having the best and the

most intriguing fibers first and has given us a truly high-fashion approach to hand knitting.

Our professional respect has deepened to a close personal friendship over the years, and again, Stacy has been unfailingly supportive. He has broadened our view by exposing us to the creative process of developing new fibers and has even let us take part in the process itself.

Without exception, Stacy has been the first to step forward with ideas to help make our business more successful. He has made connections with individuals who have provided incredible inspiration, and he also helped ensure the success of our first book by marketing it through his own company. He has been our most ardent supporter and, on occasion, most severe critic.

Through it all, Stacy's humor, honesty, and generosity have given us a model to emulate and a true sense of gratitude for the power of genuine friendship. For all of the invaluable help, challenges, and support you have given us over the years, Stacy, we dedicate this book, with love, to you!

Photo: (left to right) **back row:** Carol Simmons, Dinny Brones; **center row:** Ola Sankiewicz, Stacy O'Hara, Yiming Zhi, Elizabeth Elmer, and Ingrid Guldenmann; **front row:** Lindy Phelps, Julie Harris, Rose Mueller, Roxanne Gallagher, and Beryl Hiatt; **not pictured:** Tanya Parieaux

ACKNOWLEDGMENTS

"For all that has been, thanks! For all that will be, YES!"
—AUTHOR UNKNOWN

For those of you who have been in our shop, it is, we're certain, very clear that the real secret to our success is our remarkable staff. We'd like to give special thanks to Elizabeth for her creativity and eye for detail in helping to style the photography for this book. Each member of our "Tricoter Family" plays a unique role—the talents are varied, but the passion and compassion are the common threads that hold us all together!

CONTENTS

The Tricoter Archives

Why a Men's Book?

We were thrilled and flattered at the response to *Simply Beautiful Sweaters* when it was first published in the summer of 1999. Over the past year, we have gotten literally hundreds of letters, e-mails, and phone calls from knitters around the country and a few from around the world, thanking us for a book that made knitting easy, understandable, and *fun*.

Many had given up knitting, frustrated that the sweaters they knit never fit the person they were intended for, or dismayed by the closet full of unfinished projects that had left them hopelessly confused.

The unifying theme in all of the correspondence was the excitement of success! Another was very often a question: "What are you working on for the next book?"

We considered a number of possibilities but kept coming back to the idea of a men's sweater book because *we* had a tremendously difficult time finding classic, easy, wearable sweater patterns that the men in our lives really liked. We found many beautiful, complex, twenty-four-bobbin masterpieces and intricate, charted multipattern brainteasers that were designed for size 2 or 3 needles. (And yes, we've knit a few of those ourselves. They were usually labors of love early in a relationship that were met with a look of terror rather than gratitude by a boyfriend who saw it as a not-so-subtle mark of commitment—but more on that subject later!)

What we couldn't find were the kind of patterns that we've included in this book: classic silhouettes in beautiful yarns, to knit on relatively large needles. These are the sweaters we love to knit and that we hope will appeal to both men and women. Most have a twist of some sort: an interesting stitch or cable, occasional color work, or a design detail that makes them more interesting to knit—and to wear!

As we started to gather material for our manuscript, we realized that the sweaters we chose all had stories attached to them. They had all been designed for different men in our lives. For us, the true joy of knitting is not so much in the completion, but in the planning, selection, and process of knitting. The wonderful memories attached to each of these sweaters has as much to do with the design of a particular sweater—reflecting the very personal style of the man for whom it was knit—the swatching and reworking of the pattern to make it come out just perfectly, and the selection of the perfect combination of yarns, as it does with the pleasure of its recipient upon completion.

For us, knitting is not a craft or a hobby—it is a passion, a way of life around which we plan all other activities. Some have likened it to a sickness; for the two of us, it is our escape and our meditation. Our hope in writing this book is that it will ignite the same passion that we share and create as much joy as we have found in the very personal process of making something for someone we love.

A Few Words About Men

"Some men need a lot of room (like Montana)."
—AUTHOR UNKNOWN

Once we decided to do a book that would contain our favorite men's sweaters, we

women, and a few men, who come to Tricoter to knit. What we have found is that for many men, hand-knit garments (anything from mufflers to socks to sweaters) are perceived as so personal that they are overwhelming.

A friend of ours spent several sleepless nights sitting up to finish a sweater she was knitting for her boyfriend of several years to wear to a major presentation in another state. She finished it the night before his presentation, FedExed it to him, and never heard from him again!

We've both dated men over the years who vanished into thin air after being presented with our hand-knit "labors of love." It took us some time to make the connection, but after so many stories from knitters around the country, we now counsel women in new relationships to go slowly when considering knitting for their men.

We've both met men now who have convinced us that when the attraction is genuine, The Hex can be overcome. Jay and Larry love the sweaters we knit for them, but they often complain that they only get to "visit" their sweaters when they come to the shop. You see, while we, too, love the sweaters we knit for them, we also realize that they help sell yarn when they're displayed in our store.

realized that these sweaters are by no means impersonal objects. Each sweater that we selected (although it may have been reknit many times in any number of fibers, colors, and sizes for men we've never met) is very personally connected to a particular man in our lives.

These men are as varied as the sweaters themselves, but the connecting thread is their love of color, texture, luxurious fibers, and, of course, us. We were very wary about knitting for men in the beginning. We had heard stories about "The Sweater Hex," and we knew women who had been foolish enough to scoff at The Hex and were now paying the price.

We've done a fair amount of informal research on this subject over the years. We have a rich source in the variety of

Determining Dimensions and Adapting Men's Patterns for Women

We have found that men *love* to be a part of the design process. Because knitting a sweater is a significant commitment of both time and money, it makes sense to make certain that the sweater you're knitting is one that *he'll* be comfortable wearing.

It's a good idea to get your hands on a favorite garment, one that is similar in scale to the sweater you're planning to knit. It can be a sweater, sweatshirt, or jacket; the important criteria is that he likes the way it fits. This will help ensure that the final product is one that he will really feel comfortable wearing. It will also give you a clear idea about how he likes his clothes to fit. Some men prefer sweaters that fit close and are tailored; others like a looser and more casual feel. Careful measurements taken from a favorite garment will be your best guide in sizing the sweater properly.

If a garment is not available for exact sizing, find out his general size for cloth-ing bought "off the rack." Look at the way he dresses—does he like clothing that is fitted and close to the body or looser and more relaxed and sportier? Chances are, he'll want his sweater to fit the same way.

We've had a lot of interest in a sec-ond book from those who purchased our first one, *Simply Beautiful Sweaters*. Several women voiced similar concerns when they heard that this book was a men's sweater book: "I don't have a man in my life to knit for!" The good news is that any of these sweaters can be easily adapted for women. And truthfully, some of the sweaters we love to wear most are those we've knit for our men.

The primary differences between men's and women's sweaters are the scale, and the fact that the buttons are on oppo-site sides on cardigans. In our first book, we sized our sweater patterns in small, medium, and large. In this book, we have added extra-large. In designing sweaters in our store, we have found that a men's size small is generally comparable to a women's size medium.

It is always most important to go by actual dimensions, so don't be put off by the title of the book. The best sweater for you is the one you love most. There are no hard-and-fast rules.

Knitting Your Swatch

This is the most creative part of knitting your sweater. We're always surprised to hear customers complain about taking the time to knit a swatch. For us, this is the most exciting point: feeling the yarn, finding out what works, learning how certain stitches show off the beauty of a particular yarn while others get lost in the texture or color, deciding what needle size makes the yarn look and feel best, and discovering what colors work—or don't work—next to others.

Combinations that look beautiful together on a tray may have a different feel when knit in various combinations. Knitting swatches is your opportunity to play with color. Cast on twenty stitches or so, and don't be afraid to try unusual combinations or add a color that you normally wouldn't consider.

Your swatch is also your opportunity to explore new ground, to experiment outside your comfort zone. There is very

little lost over twenty stitches. It is much less painful than tearing out 8" of painstaking knitting on a sweater when you realize that the total color repeat you selected doesn't look the way you envisioned. Swatching is your chance to explore new stitches, to test new techniques. Find out what kinds of stitches you enjoy working with and which ones are too confusing or difficult to execute on the yarns you've chosen. As a rule, cotton and linen yarns have very little give, whereas wool, cashmere, and many blends are much more pliable or forgiving. It is important not to "force" a swatch (by stretching or squishing it) just to get a gauge. Remember that when it all comes together—the yarn, the stitches, the pattern—it will look and feel right to you. If this isn't happening after a few tries, add a new yarn or a different stitch—or look for a different pattern altogether. It is important to love your swatch first. If you burn out on the swatch, you can be sure you won't enjoy knitting a whole project based on it.

While knitting is not an exact science, it certainly shouldn't be a random shot in the dark either. When you approach it with some basic tools, it is an easy-to-estimate and simple-to-adjust process. Knitting a swatch to determine your gauge is the first critical step.

Determining Your Gauge

Gauge, or tension, is the most important factor in creating sweaters that really fit. All patterns are based on a specific number of stitches and rows per inch. If your knitting does not match those specifications, your garment will not fit properly.

To determine gauge, knit a sample swatch at least 4" wide and 4" long with the yarn and needles you will use for your garment. Work the specified pattern stitch to check the gauge; if no pattern is given, work the swatch in stockinette stitch. If the pattern is complex (color work or cables), work a larger swatch, perhaps 6" to 8" square.

To measure the swatch, lay it flat. Place a tape measure parallel to a row of stitches and count the number of stitches (including fractions of inches) that make 4". Divide the number of stitches in the 4" swatch by 4 to get the number of stitches per inch. This is your gauge.

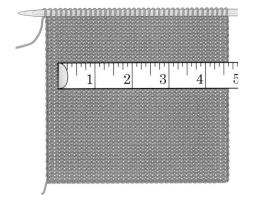

Compare this gauge to the one specified in your pattern. If your swatch has too few stitches, your work is too loose; try again with smaller needles. If your swatch has too many stitches, your work is too tight; try larger needles or a different yarn. You are ready to begin knitting when your gauge matches the one specified in the pattern.

You can bind off the stitches and use the swatch to test the washability and colorfastness of the yarn(s), save it in a notebook for future reference, or undo the knitting and reuse the yarn.

The next step is to take your gauge (the number of stitches per inch) and multiply that by the number of inches of width you want your finished garment to measure. As you knit, lay your work flat without stretching it; measure every few inches to see if your gauge has changed. When knitting on straight needles, it is important to stop halfway across the row so you can lay your work completely flat to measure it.

Checking Your Gauge

It is important to continue to measure your garment every few inches to ensure that it remains on gauge. This is particularly important if you set your work down for extended periods of time between knitting. Your tension may vary as your life changes. It may be tighter when you are tense, looser when you are more relaxed. Measure the length of your work by holding it upright. Let it hang as it would if it were being worn.

Remember to measure both the length and width of the piece. To measure an area that has been shaped, such as an armhole or sleeve, measure perpendicular to the bottom edge by laying a straight edge horizontally across the garment, even with the first row of bound-off stitches. From that straight edge, measure vertically to the lower edge of the knitting needle. On a sleeve, measure along the center of the sleeve; do not measure along the slanted side edge.

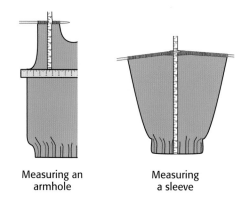

Measuring an armhole

Measuring a sleeve

It is relatively simple to adjust your pattern, increasing or decreasing a couple of stitches at this point. This is a habit you should get into and continue to practice throughout all of your knitting. To compensate for a slight variance from the original pattern, the number of stitches on the front of a garment may vary slightly from the back. However, by the time you are ready for neck and shoulder shaping, your front and back must match. They should have the same number of stitches and the same shoulder shaping.

Because we approach knitting from a very visual perspective, we find it helps to sketch a sweater in the design phase. This helps us visualize the scale and such specific design elements as the placement of striping or pockets. This is the reason we devised the pattern forms we use in the store when we create a pattern with our customers.

The forms reflect the basic shape of the actual piece that you are knitting. On our actual store pattern forms, we have a place for name and phone number (in case you misplace the form), and a place to record your specific gauge, needle sizes, and amount of yarn used. This is an invaluable reference, not only while you are knitting the sweater, but also in the event that you want to knit a similar sweater in the future.

The measurements for the total length of the garment appear at the far right side of the page; next to them are the incremental measurements for ribbing and lower-body lengths, armhole depth, and shoulder shaping. Throughout the directions you will see a set of numbers in brackets; for example, [71 (80, 86) sts; 20 (22, 24)" wide]. This indicates the number of stitches you should have on your needle and how wide your work should be at a particular point in the process.

The pattern should be read from bottom to top. The initial needle size and the number of stitches to cast on for the ribbing or bottom of the garment are indicated at the bottom of the page. As you read up the form, we indicate the points at which you should change needle sizes, any increases and/or decreases, and pattern or stitch information for the body of the garment. Be sure to measure your work often to ensure proper fit and to avoid having to rip out your work. If, after knitting several inches, you find that your sweater is slightly too large or too

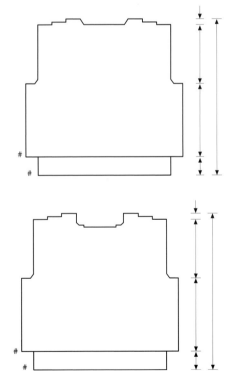

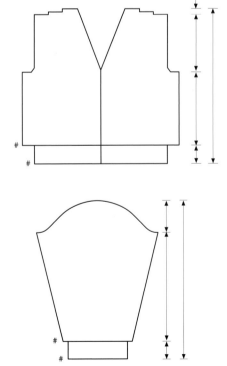

small, it is not too late to add or decrease a couple of stitches. Note any changes directly on the form to remind yourself to make the front(s) slightly wider or narrower to compensate. Or, if necessary, recalculate your gauge and begin again.

On patterns that require armhole shaping, we specify the number, type, and frequency of decreases to achieve the desired shaping. On most sweater backs, the back neck shaping and shoulder shaping happens at the same time. We believe this is critical to ensure proper fit. In the case of deep V-necks on sweater fronts, it may be necessary to begin neck shaping decreases either slightly sooner or later than the armhole shaping.

On many sweater fronts, the neck shaping occurs several inches before or almost at the same time as the shoulder shaping. It is helpful to use your sweater back as a guide for shaping the front; remember, the front and back need to line up, so measure often to ensure proper length.

Sleeve patterns are also read from bottom to top. On most of our sweater patterns, we shape the sleeve cap. This is the portion that connects the sleeve to the body of the sweater. Proper cap shaping ensures that the sleeve fits into the armhole as neatly as possible.

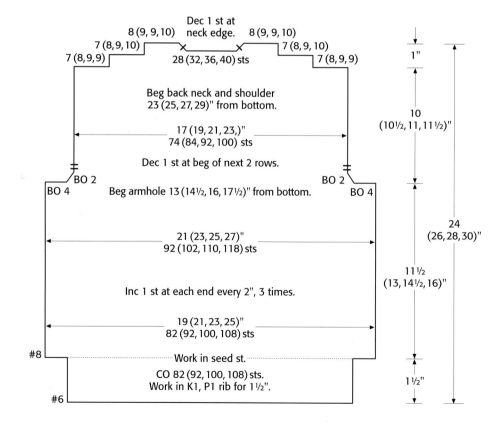

Knitting Terms and Abbreviations

beg—begin or beginning

BO—bind off

C2B—cable to back

slip 2 sts (knitwise) onto cable needle and hold to back of work; knit the next 2 sts; knit the 2 sts off the cable needle

C2F—cable to front

slip 2 sts (knitwise) onto cable needle and hold to front of work; knit the next 2 sts; knit the 2 sts off the cable needle

CO—cast on

cont—continue or continuing

dec—decrease or decreasing

noted by "—", "/", or "\" symbols on edges or at neckline

EOR—every other row

garter st—garter stitch

knit every row

inc—increase or increasing

K—knit

K2tog—knit 2 stitches together

M1—make one (see "Increasing Your Stitches" on page 130)

MC—main color

P—purl

PSSO—pass slipped stitch over

rep—repeat

rib—ribbing

RS—right side

seed st—seed stitch

knit 1 stitch, purl 1 stitch, offset stitches on next row

st/sts—stitch/stitches

St st—stockinette stitch

knit 1 row, purl 1 row, repeat these 2 rows

sl—slip

as if to purl unless otherwise noted

wyib—with yarn in back

wyif—with yarn in front

WS—wrong side

THE SPORTING LIFE

"Sports do not build character. They reveal it." —HEYWOOD HALE BROUN

Here in the Pacific Northwest, sports are an integral part of everyday life. Our relatively moderate climate lends itself to outdoor activities throughout the year, and sweaters are more or less a part of the "uniform" for almost every sport. We've included one of our longtime favorite novelty patterns—golf club covers—in this section as well. These are the ultimate gift for any golfer!

FRANK'S SWEATER

This sweater is dedicated to a very dear friend of ours who would have loved and improved the sweater just by wearing it. Frank was an incredibly beautiful man—dark and handsome—and so charming that one was immediately drawn to him. Our fondest shared memory of Frank is of a drive along the narrow, often steep road along the shores of Lake Cuomo in northern Italy on our way to Bellagio several summers ago. Frank slid from one side of the bus to the other exclaiming about each beautiful old estate or breathtaking view that he knew to be just around the next corner, as we hung on for dear life, praying that we wouldn't fly off the road! Frank's love of beauty was surpassed only by his need to share it, and we count ourselves lucky to have enjoyed the incredible beauty of that drive with him.

SIZES

Small/Medium (Large/X-Large)
Finished Chest: 44 (52)"
Finished Length: 25 (28)"

MATERIALS

Use a bulky yarn that knits at 4.0 sts to
1" in St st.
25 (28) skeins of Filatura di Crosa Clara,
100% merino extra fine wool, each
approximately 49 yds [1225 (1372) yds
total], in the following colors:
18 (20) skeins in Black #16 (color A)
7 (8) skeins in Olive #13 (color B)
#10½ and #10¾ needles
Stitch holders

GAUGE

16 sts and 20 rows = 4" in pattern stitch on
#10¾ needles
Always check gauge before starting sweater.
Increase or decrease needle size to obtain
correct gauge.

RIB PATTERN

Row 1 (with A): K1 (edge st), *P1, K1*; rep
from * to *, end P1, K1 (edge st).
Row 2 (with A and B): K1 with both, *K1 with
A, K1 with B*; rep from * to *, end K1
with A, K1 with both.
Row 3 (with A): Rep row 1.
Row 4 (with A): K1, *K1, P1*; rep from * to
*, end K1, K1.
Row 5 (with A and B): K1 with both, *P1 with
A, P1 with B*; rep from * to *, end P1
with A, K1 with both.
Row 6 (with A): Rep row 4.
Rep rows 1–6.

PATTERN 1

Stockinette Stitch

Row 1: Knit with A.
Row 2: Purl with A.
Row 3: K1 with both (edge st), *K1 with A,
K1 with B*; rep from * to *, end K1 with
both (edge st).
Row 4: Purl with A.
Row 5: Knit with A.
Row 6: K1 with both, *P1 with A, P1 with B*;
rep from * to *, end K1 with both.
Repeat rows 1–3. (End Pattern 1 with either
row 3 or row 6.)

PATTERN 2

Stockinette Stitch

Row 1: Knit with A.

Row 2: Purl with A.
Row 3: K1 with both (edge st), *K3 with A,
K1 with B*; rep from * to *, end K1 with
both (edge st).
Row 4: Knit with A.
Row 5: Purl with A.
Row 6: K1 with both, K1 with A, K1 with B,
K3 with A, K1 with B; rep from * to *,
end K1 with both (this creates the "offset"
in the pattern).
Rep rows 1–6.

BACK

1. With #10½ needles, CO 81 (95) sts.
Work in rib pattern for 3". End on
WS row.

2. With RS facing and #10¾ needles,
beg pattern 1.

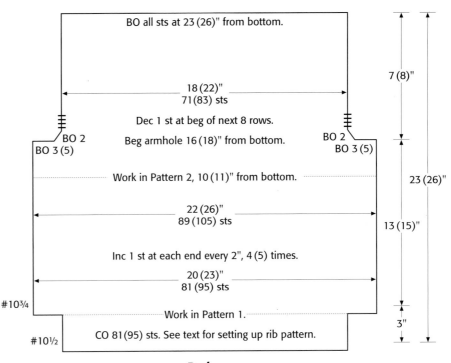

BO all sts at 23 (26)" from bottom.

18 (22)"
71 (83) sts

7 (8)"

Dec 1 st at beg of next 8 rows.

BO 2
BO 3 (5)

Beg armhole 16 (18)" from bottom.

BO 2
BO 3 (5)

Work in Pattern 2, 10 (11)" from bottom.

23 (26)"

22 (26)"
89 (105) sts

13 (15)"

Inc 1 st at each end every 2", 4 (5) times.

20 (23)"
81 (95) sts

#10¾

Work in Pattern 1.

#10½

CO 81 (95) sts. See text for setting up rib pattern.

3"

Back

23

- Inc 1 st at each end every 2" 4 (5) times [89 (105) sts; 22 (26)" wide].
- Cont in pattern 1 until work measures 10 (11)" from bottom.

3. Switch to pattern 2 and cont until work measures 16 (18)" from bottom.

4. Beg armhole shaping:
   - BO 3 (5) sts at beg of next 2 rows.
   - BO 2 sts at beg of next 2 rows.
   - Dec 1 st at beg of next 8 rows [71 (83) sts; 18 (22)" wide].

5. Cont in pattern 2 until work measures 23 (26)" from bottom.

6. BO all sts.

FRONT

1. Work the front exactly the same as the back until work measures 22 (25)" from bottom.

2. Beg front neck shaping:
   - Work first 28 (34) sts. BO center 15 sts and finish row. Turn work.
   - Work across row. Turn work.
   - BO 4 sts and finish row. Turn work.
   - Work across row. Turn work.
   - BO 2 sts and finish row. Turn work.
   - Work across row. Turn work.
   - Dec 1 st at neck edge EOR 2 times.
   - BO last 20 (26) sts.

3. Complete front neck shaping:
   - Join yarn at neck edge. BO 4 sts and finish row. Turn work.
   - Work across row. Turn work.

- BO 2 sts. Finish row. Turn work.
- Work across row. Turn work.
- Dec 1 st at neck edge EOR 2 times.
- BO last 20 (26) sts.

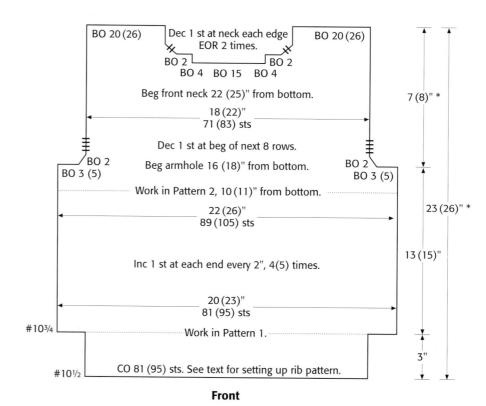

BO 20 (26)   Dec 1 st at neck each edge EOR 2 times.   BO 20 (26)

BO 2   BO 2

BO 4   BO 15   BO 4

Beg front neck 22 (25)" from bottom.

18 (22)"
71 (83) sts

Dec 1 st at beg of next 8 rows.

Beg armhole 16 (18)" from bottom.

BO 2
BO 3 (5)

BO 2
BO 3 (5)

Work in Pattern 2, 10 (11)" from bottom.

22 (26)"
89 (105) sts

Inc 1 st at each end every 2", 4 (5) times.

20 (23)"
81 (95) sts

#10¾

Work in Pattern 1.

#10½   CO 81 (95) sts. See text for setting up rib pattern.

7 (8)" *

23 (26)" *

13 (15)"

3"

Front

* Measurements do not include shoulder and neckband.

SLEEVES

Note: *The single increases (M1) on the three sections of the sleeve are to create a selvage edge for sewing the three sections together later.*

1. With #10½ needles, CO 41 (45) sts and work in rib pattern for 3". Inc 1 st in center of last row of rib.

2. With RS facing, switch to #10¾ needles and pattern 2; work first 14 (16) sts.
   ♦ Inc (M1), then place rest of row [28 (30) sts] on a stitch holder—keeping 15 (17) sts on your right-hand needle—and complete right-hand one-third of sleeve:
   ♦ Work in pattern 2, inc 1 st at outside edge every 6 rows 13 (15) times [28 (32) sts; 7 (8)" wide].
   ♦ Cont in pattern stitch until work measures 19 (21)" from bottom.

3. Complete cap shaping for this one-third of sleeve:
   ♦ BO 4 (6) sts at outside edge EOR twice.
   ♦ BO 5 sts at outside edge EOR 4 times.

4. Join yarn at outside edge of left side of sleeve (just above cuff) and purl first 14 (16) sts off stitch holder, working in pattern 2.
   ♦ Inc (M1) st and turn work (leaving center 14 sts on stitch holder).
   ♦ Complete left one-third of sleeve, working same as right one-third but reversing shaping.

5. Now go to center 14 sts of sleeve, and with RS facing, join color B yarn at right side of stitch holder.
   ♦ Inc in first st and knit next 6 sts.
   ♦ Switch to color A and knit next 7 sts, inc in last st (16 sts total—8 sts of each color).
   ♦ Cont working these 16 sts, switching colors every 8 sts for 9 more rows.
   ♦ Reverse colors A and B for next 10 rows.
   ♦ Rep this 10-row pattern 8 (9) more times. Work should now measure 20 (21)" from bottom.

6. With RS facing, switch to #10½ needles and cont this 10-row checkerboard for 20 (30) more rows.

7. At this point, separate right and left squares and cont to alternate colors as before. (You are now creating the front and back neckband for the sweater.)
   ♦ Work 15 more rows for back neck half and 25 more rows for front neck half, changing colors every 10 rows as before on both sides. You will end with half squares; place these sts on stitch holders.

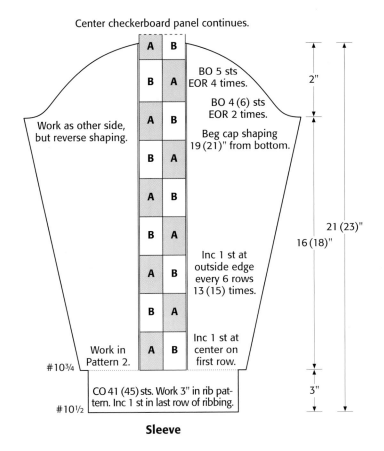

Center checkerboard panel continues.

BO 5 sts EOR 4 times.

2"

BO 4 (6) sts EOR 2 times.

Beg cap shaping 19 (21)" from bottom.

Work as other side, but reverse shaping.

21 (23)"

16 (18)"

Inc 1 st at outside edge every 6 rows 13 (15) times.

Work in Pattern 2.

Inc 1 st at center on first row.

#10¾

CO 41 (45) sts. Work 3" in rib pattern. Inc 1 st in last row of ribbing.

#10½

3"

Sleeve

FINISHING

1. Sew sleeves: place 3 sections of sleeve flat and ease checkerboard into place, pinning as you work.

2. Place front and back of sweater as shown below, along with sleeves and neckband strips.
   ◆ Pin sleeve caps to front and back of sweater.
   ◆ Pin front and back neckbands to sweater body so that half squares meet at center front and back of neckline.

3. Connect center back neck seam where 2 half squares meet:
   ◆ With WS facing and #10½ needles, pick up 1 st from left-hand half square and 1 st from right-hand half square and knit the two together as one.
   ◆ Cont with rest of sts along both edges, binding off as you go until both halves of back neck are joined.

Note: *If you have not tried this technique before, it's a good idea to practice with sample swatches before working on the sweater.*

4. Rep for front neck.

5. Sew all seams as pinned. Sew side and sleeve seams.

6. Block sweater to desired measurements. Because of the sewing required on the sleeves, turn sweater inside out and press firmly along seams to flatten them.

7. Stabilize neck front and back.

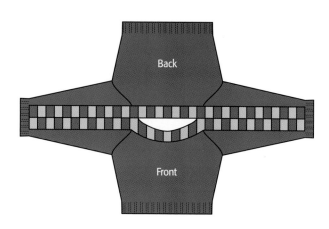

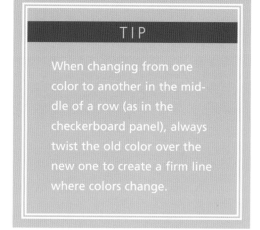

TIP

When changing from one color to another in the middle of a row (as in the checkerboard panel), always twist the old color over the new one to create a firm line where colors change.

JAY'S GOLF VEST

Seattle has arguably some of the best "sweater weather" in the country. It is temperate enough most winters that a good, heavy sweater is the perfect alternative to a coat. During the summer, the air cools down just enough to require a sweater in the evenings. The real challenge comes when you are involved in a sport that requires outdoor layering against the chill but you don't want the restriction of movement that a heavy sweater sometimes causes. I designed this vest for my boyfriend, Jay, to wear on late fall afternoons on the golf course. It provides a warm layer to insulate as he plays, without inhibiting his movement for those crucial swings. It has become not only his favorite vest for golf, but also his cold-weather "uniform." The original vest got so much wear that it wasn't in any shape to photograph, so this is the second generation. We've had as many women as men make this sweater for themselves!—Lindy

SIZES

Small, (Medium, Large, X-Large)
Finished Chest: 42 (46, 50, 54)"
Finished Length: 27 (28, 29, 30)"

MATERIALS

Use a yarn that knits at 2.25 sts to 1".
6 (6, 7, 8) skeins of Horstia Marroko, 100%
    wool, each approximately 88 yds [528
    (528, 616, 704) yds total]
For optional pockets: 1 skein (70 yds mini-
    mum) of a similar color yarn that knits at 4
    sts to 1" on #8 needles for pocket lining
#13 and #15 needles
#13 circular needle (20")
#8 needles (for optional pockets)
Size K crochet hook
29 (30, 31, 32)" separating zipper

GAUGE

9 sts and 12 rows = 4" in St st on #13
    needles
Always check gauge before starting sweater.
    Increase or decrease needle size to obtain
    correct gauge.

BACK

1. With #13 needles, CO 50 (54, 58, 62)
   sts. Work in K1, P1 rib for 3".

2. On last row of rib (WS row), inc as
   follows:
   ◆ Work 11 (12, 13, 14) sts in rib.
   ◆ Inc (M1) in each of the next 4 sts.
   ◆ Work 20 (22, 24, 26) sts in rib.
   ◆ Inc (M1) in each of the next 4 sts.
   ◆ Work last 11 (12, 13, 14) sts in rib
   [58 (62, 66, 70) sts].

3. Switch to #15 needles; set up cable
   pattern on next (RS) row:
   ◆ K10 (11, 12, 13) sts, P1, K8, P1,
   K18 (20, 22, 24) sts, P1, K8, P1,
   knit last 10 (11, 12, 13) sts.

4. Work the first cable twist on row 5
   (RS row):
   ◆ K10 (11, 12, 13) sts, P1, C4B, P1,
   K18 (20, 22, 24) sts, P1, C4B, P1,
   K10 (11, 12, 13) sts.

5. Cont in pattern, twisting on every
   10th (RS) row from this point.

6. Cont until work measures 16 (16½,
   17, 17)" from bottom.

7. Beg armhole shaping:
   ◆ BO 3 (4, 4, 4) sts at beg of next 2
   rows.
   ◆ BO 2 sts at beg of next 2 rows.
   ◆ Dec 1 st at beg of next 6 rows [42
   (44, 48, 52) sts; 15 (16, 17½, 19)"
   wide].

8. Cont until work measures 26 (27, 28,
   29)" from bottom.

9. Beg back neck and shoulder shaping:
   ◆ BO first 6 (6, 6, 7) sts, dec 2 sts in
   process as follows. (This will get rid
   of 2 of the extra sts added when the
   cable was first set up.)

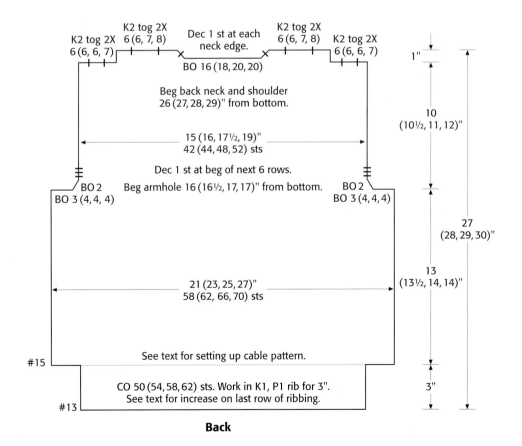

Back

– K2tog.

– K1 and BO.

– K1 and BO.

– K2tog and BO.

– For X-large, BO 1 more st, added when the cable was first set up.

♦ Knit next 7 (7, 8, 9) sts. Keeping 8 (8, 9, 10) sts on right-hand needle, BO center 16 (18, 20, 20) sts. Finish row. Turn work.

♦ BO the first 6 (6, 6, 7) sts as above. (This will get rid of 2 more of the extra sts added when the cable was first set up.) Finish row. Turn work.

♦ Dec 1 st at neck edge. Finish row. Turn work.

♦ BO last 6 (6, 7, 8) sts, dec 2 sts as above.

10. Complete back neck and shoulder shaping:

♦ Join yarn at neck edge. Dec 1 st and finish row. Turn work.

♦ BO last 6 (6, 7, 8) sts, dec 2 sts as above.

FRONTS

Work right and left fronts (refers to your right and left sides), beg with right front.

1. With #13 needles, CO 25 (27, 29, 31) sts. Work in K1, P1 rib for 3".

2. On last row of rib (WS row), inc as follows across the row:

♦ Work rib in first 11 (12, 13, 14) sts.

♦ Inc (M1) in each of next 4 sts.

♦ Work rib in last 10 (11, 12, 13) sts.

3. Switch to #15 needles, set up cable on next (RS) row:

♦ K10 (11, 12, 13) sts, P1, K8, P1, knit the last 9 (10, 11, 12) sts [29 (31, 33, 35) sts; 11 (11½, 12½, 13½)" wide].

Note: *For optional pockets, see facing page.*

4. Work first cable twist on row 5 (RS row):

♦ K10 (11, 12, 13) sts, P1, C4B, P1, K9 (10, 11, 12) sts.

5. Cont in pattern, twisting on every 10th (RS) row from this point.

6. Cont until work measures 16 (16½, 17, 17)" from bottom.

7. Beg armhole shaping:

♦ BO 3 (4, 4, 4) sts at outside edge. Finish row. Turn work.

♦ Work across row. Turn work.

♦ BO 2 sts at outside edge. Finish row. Turn work.

♦ Work across row. Turn work.

♦ Dec 1 st at outside edge EOR 3 times [21 (22, 24, 26) sts; 7½ (8, 8½, 9½)" wide].

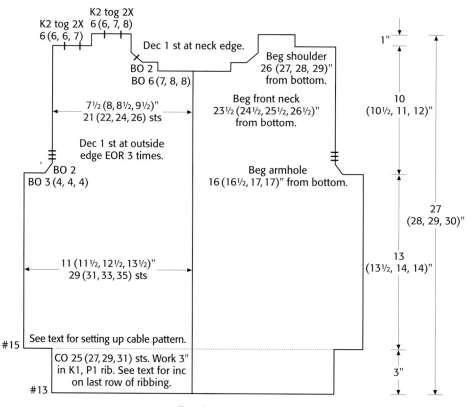

Front

8. Cont until work measures 23½ (24½, 25½, 26½)" from bottom.

9. Beg front neck shaping:
   - BO 6 (7, 8, 8) sts at neck edge. Finish the row. Turn work.
   - Work across row. Turn work.
   - BO 2 sts at neck edge. Finish row. Turn work.
   - Work across row. Turn work.
   - Dec 1 st at neck edge. Finish row. Turn work.

10. Cont until work measures 26 (27, 28, 29)" from bottom.

11. Complete shoulder shaping:
    - BO first 6 (6, 6, 7) sts, dec sts as on back. (This will get rid of 2 of the extra sts added when cable was first set up.) Finish row. Turn work.

- Work across row. Turn work.
- BO last 6 (6, 7, 8) sts, dec 2 sts as above.

12. Work left front the same as right front, but reverse the shaping.

FINISHING

1. Sew shoulder seams.

2. Collar: With RS facing and #13 circular needle, pick up a total of 43 (45, 47, 47) sts:
   - 13 (14, 15, 15) sts from right front to shoulder seam
   - 17 sts across back neck from shoulder to shoulder
   - 13 (14, 15, 15) sts from shoulder seam to left front
   - Work in K1, P1 rib for 7". Do not BO. Fold neck in half to inside of garment and sew down open sts to avoid the bulkiness of a BO row.

3. Work 1 row single crochet on each center front edge to create a finished edge.

4. Sew zipper in place.

5. Sew side and sleeve seams.

6. Armholes: With RS facing and #13 circular needle, pick up 52 (54, 56, 60) sts for each band:
   - Work 1 row in K1, P1 rib.
   - BO loosely on next row.

7. Block vest to desired measurements.

8. Stabilize back neck and shoulders.

Optional Pocket Instructions

1. At 5" from bottom, BO 3 sts at outside edge. Cont in pattern until work measures 11" from bottom:
   - CO 3 sts at outside edge (using cable cast-on) and cont as in step 6 in pattern instructions.

2. After completing both fronts and before sewing side seams, finish pockets:
   - Knit 2 pocket linings: CO 22 sts on #8 needles and work in St st for 9". BO.
   - With RS facing and #13 needles, pick up 15 sts and work 2 rows in K1, P1 rib. BO in rib.
   - Slipstitch rib edges in place.
   - Place pocket linings and slipstitch in place.

Note: *The pocket lining now becomes a part of the side seam as the sweater is sewn together.*

TIP

Leaving "live" stitches on the needle after you finish knitting the collar rather than binding them off allows you to sew the live stitches down to the pickup row stitches with much less bulk—something to consider when using chunky yarns.

GOLF CLUB COVERS

We think this is the ultimate gift for any golfer! This great set of four covers can be knit in a color to suit any golfer's taste and really adds personality to anyone's golf bag.

ONE SIZE (Makes 4 head covers)

MATERIALS

Use a yarn that knits at 5 sts to 1".

4 skeins of Filatura di Crosa Primo, 100% wool, each approximately 82 yds [330 yds total], in color A (black)

1 skein of Filatura di Crosa Primo in each of colors B, C, D, E, and F (gray, red, gold, green, and brown) [380 yds total]

#7 needles

Size 4 crochet hook

GAUGE

20 sts and 28 rows = 4" in St st on #7 needles

Always check gauge before starting project. Increase or decrease needle size to obtain correct gauge.

STRIPING SEQUENCE

Row 1: Color A

Row 2: Color B

Row 3: Color C, D, E, or F

Rep rows 1–3.

COLOR SEQUENCE

Main color A and second color B are common for all four covers. Four accent colors are divided, using one for each of the four covers.

Color A	Black	Body or background and tassels for all 4 covers
Color B	Gray	Accent color in striping and tassels for all 4 covers
Color C	Gold	Accent stripe, tassel, and number for cover 1
Color D	Red	Accent stripe, tassel, and number for cover 3
Color E	Brown	Accent stripe, tassel, and number for cover 5
Color F	Green	Accent stripe, tassel, and number for cover 7

32

To knit cover:

1. With #7 needles and color A, CO 44 sts. Work in K1, P1 rib for 28 rows, following striping sequence.

   ◆ With RS facing and color A, *K2, P2tog*; rep from * to * [33 sts].

   ◆ On next (WS) row, *K1, P2*; rep from * to *.

   ◆ On next (RS) row, *K2, P1*; rep from * to *.

   ◆ Rep last 2 rows 4 times, plus 1 more row [9 rows].

2. Beg inc: With WS facing and cont in color A, inc 1 st in first st, P2, *inc 1 st in next st, P2*; rep from * to * [44 sts].

   ◆ Work in K2, P2 rib for 6 rows.

   ◆ Knit 1 row and cont in St st to 20 rows above rib. End on WS row.

   ◆ Work next 6 rows in K2, P2 rib.

3. Beg top shaping: With RS facing and color A, *K2, P2tog*; rep from * to * [33 sts].

   ◆ Purl 1 row.

   ◆ Next row (RS): K2tog 16 times, K1 [17 sts].

   ◆ Purl 1 row.

   ◆ Next row (RS): K2tog 8 times, K1.

   ◆ Cut yarn, leaving a 24" tail.

4. To complete cover: Using crochet hook, run tail through 9 remaining sts, insert crochet hook in last st, and draw up a loop, pulling yarn tight.

   ◆ Chain 8, join with a sl st in 5th st of last knit row, chain 1, turn work.

   ◆ Slipstitch in each chain st.

   ◆ Fasten off and run yarn through 9 sts of last knit row again.

FINISHING

1. See chart for numbers: Use 2 strands of color C, D, E, or F, and stitch desired numeral at center of St st portion of cover.

2. Sew side seam, matching pattern and block.

3. Rep for remaining 3 covers.

4. Make cord: With 2 strands of color A, chain 15"; fasten off.

   ◆ Run end of cord through loops at top of 2nd and 3rd covers.

   ◆ Tie knots to secure, leaving 4½" at center of cord between covers.

   ◆ Knot first and 4th covers at each end of cord.

5. Make pompons (see page 34) for toe of each cover and sew in place.

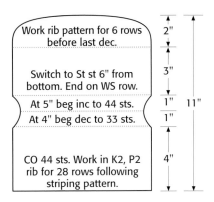

Work rib pattern for 6 rows before last dec.	2"
Switch to St st 6" from bottom. End on WS row.	3"
At 5" beg inc to 44 sts.	1"	11"
At 4" beg dec to 33 sts.	1"
CO 44 sts. Work in K2, P2 rib for 28 rows following striping pattern.	4"

Golf Club Covers

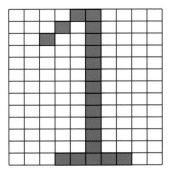

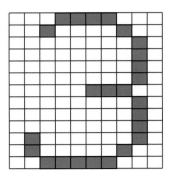

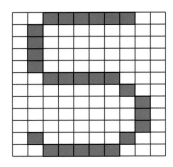

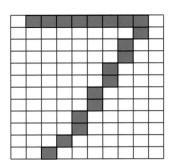

Making Pompons

1. Using 2 circular pieces of cardboard the width of the desired pompon, cut a center hole, then cut a pie-shaped wedge out of the circles.

2. Hold the 2 circles together and wrap yarn tightly around the cardboard. Carefully cut yarn around the outer edge of the cardboard.

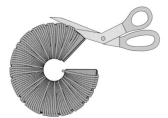
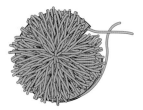

3. Tie a piece of yarn tightly between the 2 circles. Remove the cardboard and trim the pompon.

Note: *Hold finished pompon over steaming pot of water to fluff and fill it out.*

EVAN'S SWEATER

My nephew Evan is one of the very special people in my life, so when this all-state center football star asked for a hand-knit sweater as a graduation present, I was happy to knit it for him. My sister warned me that it needed to be as close to indestructible as possible to survive dorm life during his first year at college. What I wasn't quite prepared for was the time required to knit a sweater of this scale. I'm quite certain that I've knit entire throws that took less yarn! As the sweater developed, Beryl repeatedly urged me to get him in for a fitting—the sweater looked HUGE—but I wanted it to be a surprise so I continued to work from measurements of his favorite sweatshirt. When he opened it on graduation day and immediately put it on, it fit perfectly! Evan's sweater is our Large/X-Large.—Lindy

SIZES

Small/Medium (Large/X-Large)
Finished Chest: 52, (64)"
Finished Length: 25 (28)"

MATERIALS

Use a yarn that knits at 3.5 sts to 1".
18 (19) skeins of Karabella Softig, 100% cotton, each approximately 88 yds [1584, 1672 yds total]
#9 and #10 needles

GAUGE

14 sts and 16 rows = 4" in pattern stitch using #10 needles
Always check gauge before starting sweater. Increase or decrease needle size to obtain correct gauge.

PATTERN STITCH

Row 1 (RS): Purl across row.
Row 2 (WS): K1, P1.
Rep these 2 rows.

BACK

1. With #9 needles, CO 74 (88) sts. Work in K1, P1 rib for 2". Inc 1 st in last row of rib.

2. Switch to #10 needles and work in pattern stitch, inc 1 st every 4 rows 8 (11) times [91 (111) sts; 26 (32)" wide].

3. Cont in pattern stitch until work measures 13½ (15½)" from bottom. End with WS row.

4. Set up border for triangle chest pattern: With RS facing, work 6 rows in garter st.

5. Follow chart for triangle pattern.

6. Work 6 rows in garter st, ending with a WS row.

7. Cont in St st until work measures 23½ (26½)" from bottom.

8. Beg back neck and shoulder shaping:
    ◆ BO first 10 (13) sts, knit next 22 (27) sts, BO center 27 (31) sts. Finish row. Turn work.
    ◆ BO first 10 (13) sts. Finish row. Turn work.

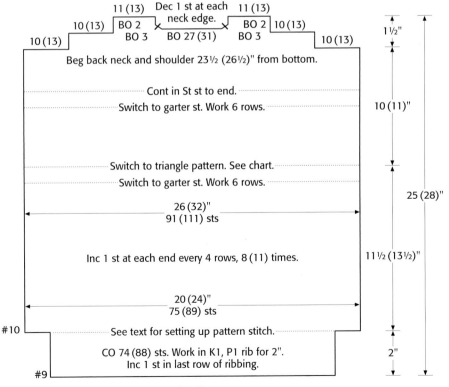

Back

- Work across row. Turn work.
- Dec 1 st at neck edge. Finish row. Turn work.
- Work across row. Turn work.
- BO 10 (13) sts. Finish row. Turn work.
- Work across row. Turn work.
- BO last 11 (13) sts.

9. Complete back neck and shoulder shaping:
- Join yarn at neck edge. Dec 1 st and finish row. Turn work.
- BO 10 (13) sts. Finish row. Turn work.
- Work across row. Turn work.
- BO last 11 (13) sts.

FRONT

1. Work the front exactly the same as back until work measures 22½ (25½)" from bottom.

2. Beg front neck shaping:
- Knit first 37 (45) sts. BO center 17 (21) sts and finish row. Turn work.
- Work back to neck edge. Turn work.
- BO 3 sts. Finish row. Turn work.
- Work across row. Turn work.
- BO 2 sts. Finish row. Turn work.
- Work across row. Turn work.
- Dec 1 st at neck edge. Finish row. Turn work.

3. Begin shoulder shaping:
- BO first 10 (13) sts at outside edge. Finish row. Turn work.
- Work across row. Turn work.
- BO first 10 (13) sts. Finish row. Turn work.
- Work across row. Turn work.
- BO last 11 (13) sts.

4. Complete front neck and shoulder shaping:
- Join yarn at neck edge and complete left side the same as right side, but reverse shaping.

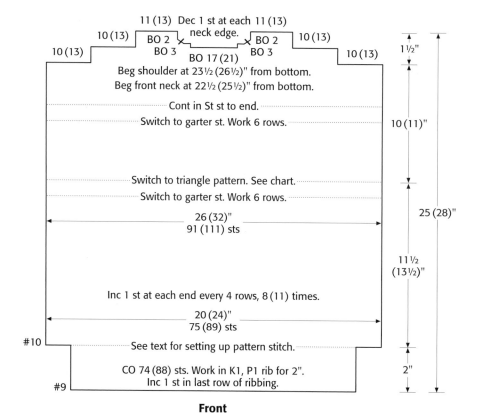

Front

SLEEVES

1. With #9 needles, CO 34 (38) sts and work in K1, P1 rib for 2".
   - Inc 4 sts evenly across last row of rib.
2. Switch to #10 needles and work in pattern stitch; inc 1 st at each end every 3 rows 16 (18) times [70 (78) sts; 19 (21)" wide].
3. Cont in pattern stitch until work measures 16 (18)" from bottom.
4. Beg cap shaping:
   - BO 8 (9) sts at beg of next 6 rows.
   - BO last 22 (24) sts.

FINISHING

1. Sew shoulder seams.
2. Complete neckband: With RS facing and #9 needles, pick up a total of 72 (76) sts:
   - Pick up 42 (44) sts across front neck.
   - Pick up 30 (32) sts across back neck.
   - Work 3 rows in K1, P1 rib; BO on 4th row.
3. Sew in sleeves. Sew side and sleeve seams.
4. Block sweater to desired measurements.
5. Stabilize back neck and shoulders.

TIP

Even though the front and back are knit separately, we found it was easier to use a circular needle than straight needles on this sweater because of the size and weight of the yarn and the number of stitches for each piece. This is also a good idea when traveling because circular needles take up less space, and there is less chance of disturbing the traveler next to you.

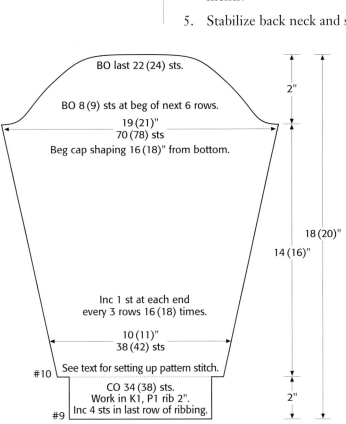

Sleeve

Sizes small and medium

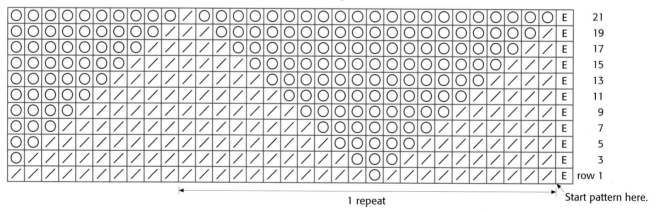

Sizes large and extra large

/ Knit   O Purl   E Edge stitch

Note: on all even-numbered rows (WS),
work sts as they face you.

LARRY'S CABLED CASHMERE PULLOVER

One of the most rewarding side effects of knitting is the calming, centering effect that it has on most knitters. I am quite certain that Beryl's fiancé, Larry, realized this early in their relationship and has used this to his advantage—judging by the number of beautiful sweaters in his closet!

An avid gardener and cook as well as a knitter, Beryl can spin herself into a frenzy on weekends. Generally up at dawn to get the first of the sprinklers going while the espresso machine is warming up for her first latte, Beryl can be found selecting herbs from her pots with a watering wand in one hand while dialing the portable phone with the other as she calls me to confirm ingredients for a soup she is planning for later in the day. By the time Larry rises for the day at seven or so, she is into the fifth or sixth project of the day. Being a slow, quiet riser by nature, he has learned that the most effective defense against this flurry of activity is to get her to stop and knit for an hour or so.

This sweater was one of the last to be finished for our book. With our manuscript deadline in early fall, the same time that fall yarns are hitting our shop and business is really starting to hum, the frenzy had reached a high. I think it's only a slight overstatement to say that this might have been the sweater that kept Beryl sane. The calming process of sitting down to knit and the soft luxury of the cashmere and wool fiber combined to make this sweater one of the relaxing pleasures in a time of turbulence!—Lindy

SIZES

Small (Medium, Large, X-Large)
Finished Chest: 42 (46, 50, 54)"
Finished Length: 24 (26, 28, 30)"

MATERIALS

Use a yarn that knits at 4.5 sts per inch in
St st.
11 (12, 12, 13) skeins of Filatura di Crosa
Cashmere Tweed, 70% wool and 30%
cashmere, each approximately 126 yds
[1386 (1512, 1512, 1638) yds total]
#6, #7, and #8 needles
Cable needle

GAUGE

21 sts and 25 rows = 4" in rib pattern on #8
needles
Always check gauge before starting sweater.
Increase or decrease needle size to obtain
correct gauge.

FRONT AND BACK CABLE/RIB PATTERN

Row 1 (WS): *K2, P4*; rep from * to *.
Row 2 (RS): Work sts as they face you.
Row 3: Rep row 1.
Row 4: P2, C2F, *P2, K4, P2, K4, P2, K4,
C2F*; rep from * to *.
Rows 5–9: Rep rows 1 and 2.
Row 10: Rep row 4.
Rows 11–15: Rep rows 1 and 2.
Row 16: Rep row 4.
Rows 17–21: Rep rows 1 and 2.
Row 22: Rep row 4.
Rows 23–27: Rep rows 1 and 2.

Row 28: P2, K4, P2, K4, P2, C2F, *P2, K4, P2,
K4, P2, K4, P2, C2F*; rep from * to *.
Rows 29–33: Rep rows 1 and 2.
Row 34: Rep row 28.
Rows 35–39: Rep rows 1 and 2.
Row 40: Rep row 28.
Rows 41–45: Rep rows 1 and 2.
Row 46: Rep row 28.
Rep rows 1–46.

Note: *Because ribbing naturally pulls in, you will need to spread your piece a bit. It should "open up" easily approximately 4" across the width of the front or back of the sweater to achieve the desired width without looking distorted.*

BACK

1. With #8 needles, CO 110 (122, 134, 146) sts. (These numbers include edge sts.) To set up pattern:
   ◆ Row 1 (WS): K1, P2, *K2, P4*; rep from * to *, end K2, P2, K1.
   ◆ Work in K4, P2 rib pattern until work measures 6" from bottom. Finish on WS row.

2. Work first 5 (11, 17, 23) sts in established rib pattern, C2F, *P2, K4, P2, K4, P2, K4, P2, C2F*; rep from * to * 4 more times. Cont in established rib pattern.

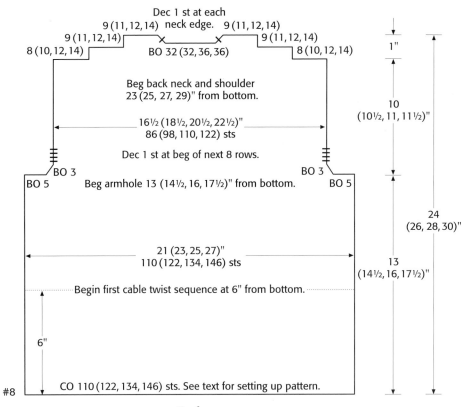

Back

♦ Work 5 rows in rib pattern; on next row, rep cable-twist row.

♦ Work 5 more rows; rep cable-twist row a 3rd time.

♦ Work 5 more rows; rep cable-twist row a 4th time.

3. Work 5 more rows; beg alternate cable-twist row:

♦ Work first 17 (23, 29, 35) sts in established rib pattern, C2F, *P2, K4, P2, K4, P2, K4 P2, C2F*; rep from * to * 3 more times. Cont in established rib pattern.

♦ Work 5 rows in rib pattern; on next row, rep cable-twist row.

♦ Work 5 more rows; rep cable-twist row a 3rd time.

♦ Work 5 more rows; rep cable-twist row a 4th time.

4. Cont in cable/rib pattern until work measures 13 (14½, 16, 17½)" from bottom [110 (122, 134, 146) sts; 21 (23, 25, 27)" wide].

5. Beg armhole shaping:

♦ BO 5 sts at beg of next 2 rows.

♦ BO 3 sts at beg of next 2 rows.

♦ Dec 1 st at beg of next 8 rows [86 (98, 110, 122) sts; 16½ (18½, 20½, 22½)" wide].

6. Cont in cable/rib pattern until work measures 23 (25, 27, 29)" from bottom.

7. Beg back neck and shoulder shaping:

♦ BO first 8 (10, 12, 14) sts. Work next 17 (22, 24, 28) sts. Keeping 18 (23, 25, 29) sts on right-hand

needle, BO center 32 (32, 36, 36) sts. Finish row. Turn work.

♦ BO first 8 (10, 12, 14) sts. Finish row. Turn work.

♦ Dec 1 st at neck edge. Finish row. Turn work.

♦ BO first 9 (11, 12, 14) sts. Finish row. Turn work.

♦ Work across row. Turn work.

♦ BO last 9 (11, 12, 14) sts.

8. Complete back neck and shoulder shaping:

♦ Join yarn at neck edge. Dec 1 st and finish row. Turn work.

♦ BO 9 (11, 12, 14) sts. Finish row. Turn work.

♦ Work across row. Turn work.

♦ BO last 9 (11, 12, 14) sts.

FRONT

1. Work the front exactly the same as the back until work measures 20½ (22½, 24½, 26½)" from bottom.

2. Beg front neck shaping:

♦ Work first 35 (41, 45, 51) sts. BO center 14 (14, 18, 18) sts. Finish row. Turn work.

♦ Work across row. Turn work.

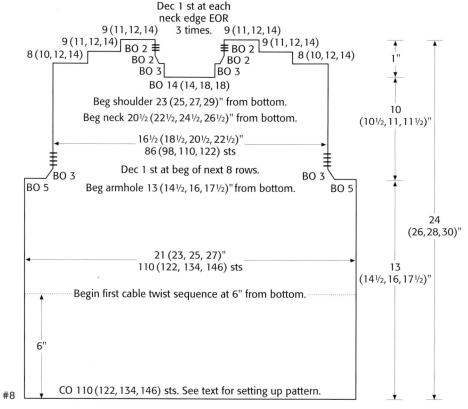

Dec 1 st at each neck edge EOR 3 times.

9 (11, 12, 14) 9 (11, 12, 14) 9 (11, 12, 14) 9 (11, 12, 14)

8 (10, 12, 14) BO 2 BO 2 8 (10, 12, 14)

BO 2 BO 2

BO 3 BO 3

BO 14 (14, 18, 18)

Beg shoulder 23 (25, 27, 29)" from bottom.
Beg neck 20½ (22½, 24½, 26½)" from bottom.

16½ (18½, 20½, 22½)"
86 (98, 110, 122) sts

Dec 1 st at beg of next 8 rows.
Beg armhole 13 (14½, 16, 17½)" from bottom.

BO 3 BO 3

BO 5 BO 5

21 (23, 25, 27)"
110 (122, 134, 146) sts

Begin first cable twist sequence at 6" from bottom.

6"

#8   CO 110 (122, 134, 146) sts. See text for setting up pattern.

1"

10 (10½, 11, 11½)"

24 (26, 28, 30)"

13 (14½, 16, 17½)"

Front

- BO 3 sts at neck edge. Finish row. Turn work.
  - Work across row. Turn work.
  - BO 2 sts at neck edge EOR twice.
  - Work across row. Turn work.
  - Dec 1 st at neck edge EOR 3 times.

3. Cont until work measures 23 (25, 27, 29)" from bottom.

4. Beg shoulder shaping:
   - BO 8 (10, 12, 14) sts at outside edge. Finish row to neck edge. Turn work.
   - Work across row. Turn work.
   - BO 9 (11, 12, 14) sts. Finish row. Turn work.
   - Work across row. Turn work.
   - BO last 9 (11, 12, 14) sts.

5. Complete front neck shaping:
   - Join yarn at neck edge. BO 3 sts and finish row. Turn work.
   - Work across row. Turn work.
   - BO 2 sts at neck edge EOR twice.
   - Work across row. Turn work.
   - Dec 1 st at neck edge EOR 3 times.

6. Cont until work measures 23 (25, 27, 29)" from bottom.

7. Complete shoulder shaping as in step 4.

SLEEVES

1. With #7 needles, CO 46 (48, 50, 54) sts and set up rib pattern (includes edge sts):
   - **Small:** K3, *K2, P4*; rep from * to *, end K3.
     Medium: K1, P1, *K2, P4*; rep from * to *, end K2, P1, K1.
     Large: K1, P2, *K2, P4*; rep from * to *, end K2, P2, K1.
     X-Large: K1, P2, *K2, P4*; rep from * to *, end K3.
   - Work in rib pattern for 2".

2. Switch to #8 needles. Cont in rib pattern, inc 1 st at each end every 5 rows 18 (19, 20, 21) times [82 (86, 90, 96) sts; 16 (17, 18, 19)" wide].

3. Cont in pattern until work measures 18 (19, 20, 21)" from bottom.

4. Beg cap shaping:
   - BO 5 sts at beg of next 2 rows.
   - BO 3 sts at beg of next 2 rows.
   - BO 2 sts at beg of next 16 rows.
   - BO 3 sts at beg of next 6 rows.
   - BO last 16 (20, 24, 30) sts.

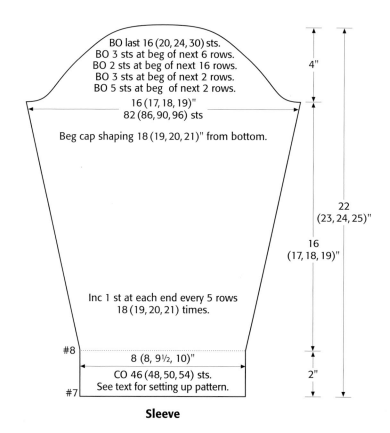

BO last 16 (20, 24, 30) sts.
BO 3 sts at beg of next 6 rows.
BO 2 sts at beg of next 16 rows.
BO 3 sts at beg of next 2 rows.
BO 5 sts at beg of next 2 rows.

16 (17, 18, 19)"
82 (86, 90, 96) sts

Beg cap shaping 18 (19, 20, 21)" from bottom.

4"

22 (23, 24, 25)"

16 (17, 18, 19)"

Inc 1 st at each end every 5 rows 18 (19, 20, 21) times.

#8

8 (8, 9½, 10)"

CO 46 (48, 50, 54) sts.
See text for setting up pattern.

#7

2"

Sleeve

FINISHING

1. Sew shoulder seams.

2. With RS facing and #7 needles, pick up a total of 90 (90, 98, 98) sts:
   - Pick up 35 (35, 40, 40) sts across back neck from shoulder to shoulder.
   - Pick up 55 (55, 58, 58) sts across front neck from shoulder to shoulder.
   - Work in K1, P1 rib for 1½". *Do not* BO. Instead, to reduce bulk, fold collar to inside of sweater and sew down "live" sts to pickup-row sts.

3. Knit separate collar:
   - With #8 needles, CO 129 (129, 137, 137) sts. Switch immediately to #6 needles and work 3 more rows in K1, P1 rib.

   - Dec 1 st at each end EOR 15 times. Collar should now measure 4" in length [99 (99, 107, 107) sts]. Again, *do not* BO.

4. Attach collar:
   - With WS facing, beg at center back neck and ease long (cast-on) edge of collar in place so that ends overlap at front neck by 8 sts to left and right of center. Pin in place as you work, then sew down.
   - Fold short side ("live" sts) to outside (staying inside collar that was picked up and knit to sweater originally) and ease into place. Carefully sew down live sts evenly around neck as close to pickup row as possible.

5. Sew in sleeves. Sew side and sleeve seams.

6. Block sweater to desired measurements.

7. Stabilize back neck and shoulders.

> **TIP**
>
> When steaming completed pieces, block finished front and back approximately 2" wider than desired finished width, since this sweater will spring back a bit as it is worn.

BY DESIGN

"Form ever follows function."—LOUIS HENRI SULLIVAN

Color and texture are the most exciting elements of design for us. Good design can be evident in the simplest of sweaters by the incorporation of these two elements. Often, the combination and placement of stitches creates an overall pattern that has a much more complex look than the actual process of knitting. The unexpected combinations of subtle colors and fibers are the secret to many of our most successful sweaters. For us, the true joy of knitting is in the limitless freedom to create!

JAY'S SILK PULLOVER

Finding beautiful, luxury yarns that are fairly durable for summer-weight men's sweaters has always been a challenge for us. Finding the colors and a style that would suit the classic taste of my boyfriend, Jay, was an additional chal- lenge. This wonderful pure silk fiber was the perfect choice. The simple slip-stitch pattern in two colors keeps the knitting interest- ing, and the modified polo neckline gives it a casual, yet tailored feel. We'd love to see it in cashmere or wool for winter!—Lindy

SIZES

Small (Medium, Large, X-Large)
Finished Chest: 42 (46, 50, 54)"
Finished Length: 24 (26, 28, 30)"

MATERIALS

Use a yarn that knits at 5.0 sts to 1".
14 (16, 17, 20) skeins of On Line Pursetta,
    100% silk, each approximately 110 yds
    [1540 (1760, 1870, 2200) yds total], in the
    following colors:
        8 (9, 9, 11) skeins of color A (khaki)
        6 (7, 8, 9) skeins for color B (ivory)
#5 and #7 needles
#5 circular needle (24")
4 buttons, approximately ¾" in diameter
Stitch holder

GAUGE

20 sts and 34 rows = 4" in pattern stitch on
    #7 needles
Always check gauge before starting sweater.
    Increase or decrease needle size to obtain
    correct gauge.

PATTERN STITCH

Three-and-One Tweed
(multiple of 4 sts, plus 3 sts, plus 2 edge sts in
    colors A and B)
CO with color B and knit 1 row.
Row 1 (RS): With A, K3, *sl 1 wyib, K3*; rep
    from * to *.
Row 2 (WS): With A, K3, *sl 1 wyif, K3*; rep
    from * to *.
Row 3: With B, K1, *sl 1 wyib, K3*; rep from
    * to *.

Row 4: With B, K1, *sl 1 wyif, K3*; rep from
    * to *.
Rep rows 1–4.

BACK

1. With #5 needles and color A, CO
    109 (117, 129, 137) sts. Work 1 row
    in K1, P1 rib.
    ◆ Switch to color B; cont in rib pat-
    tern for 1 row.
    ◆ Switch to color A; cont in rib pat-
    tern until work measures 2½" from
    bottom.

2. Switch to #7 needles and work in pat-
    tern stitch until work measures 23
    (25, 27, 29)" from bottom.

3. Beg back neck and shoulder shaping:
    ◆ BO first 12 (13, 14, 15) sts. Knit
    next 25 (27, 31, 33) sts. BO center
    35 (37, 39, 41) sts. Finish row. Turn
    work.
    ◆ BO first 12 (13, 14, 15) sts. Finish
    row. Turn work.
    ◆ Dec 1 st at neck edge. Finish row.
    Turn work.
    ◆ BO 12 (13, 15, 16) sts. Finish row.
    Turn work.
    ◆ Work across row. Turn work.
    ◆ BO last 12 (13, 15, 16) sts.

4. Complete back neck and shoulder
    shaping:
    ◆ Join yarn at neck edge. Dec 1 st
    and finish row. Turn work.

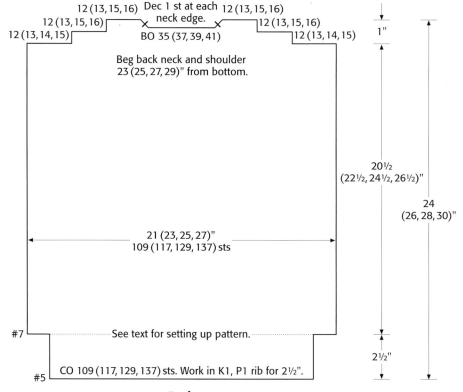

Back

- BO 12 (13, 15, 16) sts. Finish row. Turn work.
- Work across row. Turn work.
- BO last 12 (13, 15, 16) sts.

FRONT

1. Work front exactly the same as back until work measures 15 (17, 19, 21)" from bottom.

2. Now place placket and complete both fronts separately from this point:
   - Knit first 51 (55, 61, 65) sts. BO next (center) 7 sts and finish row.

Turn work. Place left front sts on stitch holder.
- Cont in pattern stitch until work measures 21½ (23½, 25½, 27½)" from bottom.

3. Beg front neck shaping:
   - BO 9 (10, 11, 12) sts at neck edge. Finish row. Turn work.
   - Work across row. Turn work.
   - BO 3 sts at neck edge. Finish row. Turn work.
   - Work across row. Turn work.
   - Dec 1 st at neck edge EOR 3 times.

4. Cont until work measures 23 (25, 27, 29)" from bottom.

5. Beg shoulder shaping:
   - BO 12 (13, 14, 15) sts. Finish row. Turn work.
   - Work across row. Turn work.
   - BO 12 (13, 15, 16) sts. Finish row. Turn work.
   - Work across row. Turn work.
   - BO last 12 (13, 15, 16) sts.

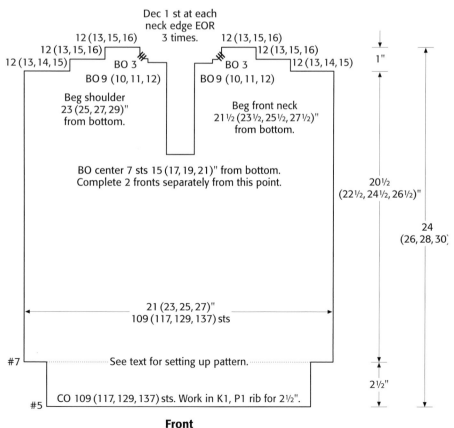

Dec 1 st at each neck edge EOR 3 times.

12 (13, 15, 16)
12 (13, 15, 16)
12 (13, 14, 15)
BO 3
12 (13, 15, 16)
12 (13, 15, 16)
12 (13, 14, 15)
BO 3
BO 9 (10, 11, 12)
BO 9 (10, 11, 12)

1"

Beg shoulder
23 (25, 27, 29)"
from bottom.

Beg front neck
21½ (23½, 25½, 27½)"
from bottom.

BO center 7 sts 15 (17, 19, 21)" from bottom.
Complete 2 fronts separately from this point.

20½
(22½, 24½, 26½)"

24
(26, 28, 30)"

21 (23, 25, 27)"
109 (117, 129, 137) sts

#7   See text for setting up pattern.

2½"

#5   CO 109 (117, 129, 137) sts. Work in K1, P1 rib for 2½".

Front

6. Joi
ple
fro

SLEEV

1. Wi
(48
P1

♦ S
ter

♦ S
ter
bot

♦ I
rib

SIZES

Small (Medium, Large, X-Large)
Finished Chest: 42 (46, 50, 54)"
Finished Length: 24 (26, 28, 30)"

MATERIALS

Use two yarns that knit together as one or
    one bulky yarn that knits at 4.25 sts to 1".
12 (12, 12, 12) skeins of Garnstudio Yarns
    Silky Tweed, 52% wool and 48% silk, each
    approximately 220 yds [2640 yds total], in
    the following colors:
        2 skeins each in red, rust, gold, wheat,
        sage, and navy
12 (12, 18, 18) total skeins of Aurora Yarns,
    Cotton Viscose, 54% cotton and 46%
    rayon, each approximately 120 yds [2160
    (2160, 2880, 2880) yds total], in the fol-
    lowing colors:
        2 (2, 3, 3) skeins each in red, rust, gold,
        wheat, sage, and navy

#6 and #8 needles
#5 circular needle (29")
Safety pin

GAUGE

17 sts and 29 rows = 4" in seed st on #8
    needles
Always check gauge before starting sweater.
    Increase or decrease needle size to obtain
    correct gauge.

STRIPING PATTERN FOR BANDS

Work 2 row stripes with both yarns of the
    same color run together as one, using all 6
    colors in one complete run in this order:
    red, rust, gold, wheat, sage, navy.

PATTERN STITCH

Work in seed st with both yarns run together
    as one, changing 1 of 2 yarns every 3 rows
    as indicated in color sequence below.
Row 1: *K1, P1; rep from * to *.
Row 2: Purl the knit sts and knit the purl sts
    as they face you.

COLOR SEQUENCE

Rows 1–3:	Red Silky Tweed	run with	Red Cotton Viscose
Rows 4–6:	Rust Silky Tweed	run with	Red Cotton Viscose
Rows 7–9:	Rust Silky Tweed	run with	Rust Cotton Viscose
Rows 10–12:	Gold Silky Tweed	run with	Rust Cotton Viscose
Rows 13–15:	Gold Silky Tweed	run with	Gold Cotton Viscose
Rows 16–18:	Wheat Silky Tweed	run with	Gold Cotton Viscose
Rows 19–21:	Wheat Silky Tweed	run with	Wheat Cotton Viscose
Rows 22–24:	Sage Silky Tweed	run with	Wheat Cotton Viscose
Rows 25–27:	Sage Silky Tweed	run with	Sage Cotton Viscose
Rows 28–30:	Navy Silky Tweed	run with	Sage Cotton Viscose
Rows 31–33:	Navy Silky Tweed	run with	Navy Cotton Viscose
Rows 34–37:	Red Silky Tweed	run with	Navy Cotton Viscose

Rep color sequence.

BACK

1. With #6 needles and red yarns run together as one, CO 82 (92, 100, 108) sts. Work in K1, P1 rib for about 1½", following striping sequence.

2. Switch to #8 needles. Work in seed st, following color sequence.
   - Inc 1 st at each end every 2" 5 times [92 (102, 110, 118) sts; 21 (23, 25, 27)" wide].

3. Cont until work measures 13 (14½, 16, 17½)" from bottom of work.

4. Beg armhole shaping:
   - BO 4 sts at beg of next 2 rows.
   - BO 2 sts at beg of next 2 rows.
   - Dec 1 st at beg of next 6 rows [74 (84, 92, 100) sts; 17 (19, 21, 23)" wide].

5. Cont until work measures 23 (25, 27, 29)" from bottom.

6. Beg back neck and shoulder shaping:
   - BO first 7 (8, 9, 9) sts; work next 16 (18, 19, 21) sts. Keeping 17 (19, 20, 22) sts on right-hand needle, BO center 28 (32, 36, 40) sts. Finish row. Turn work.

   - BO first 7 (8, 9, 9) sts. Finish row to neck edge. Turn work.
   - Dec 1 st at neck edge. Finish row. Turn work.
   - BO 7 (8, 9, 10) sts. Finish row. Turn work.
   - Work across row. Turn work.
   - BO last 8 (9, 9, 10) sts.

7. Complete back neck and shoulder shaping:
   - Join yarn at neck edge. Dec 1 st and finish row. Turn work.
   - BO 7 (8, 9, 10) sts. Finish row. Turn work.
   - Work across row. Turn work.
   - BO last 8 (9, 9, 10) sts.

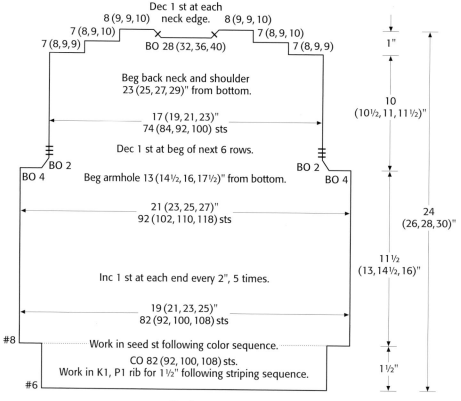

Back

FRONT

1. Work front exactly the same as back until work measures 14 (16, 18, 20)" from bottom.

2. Beg V-neck shaping: Work right front (the one you wear on your right side) first.
   ◆ Place first 45 (50, 54, 58) sts on a stitch holder.
   ◆ Place center 2 sts on a safety pin. Finish row. Turn work.
   ◆ Cont with neck dec as follows:
   Small: Dec 1 st at neck edge every 6 rows 7 times, then every 4 rows 7 times.
   Medium: Dec 1 st at neck edge every 4 rows 16 times.
   Large: Dec 1 st at neck edge every 4 rows 18 times.
   X-Large: Dec 1 st at neck edge every 4 rows 15 times, then every 2 rows 5 times [22 (25, 27, 29) sts].

3. Cont until work measures 23 (25, 27, 29)" from bottom.

4. Beg shoulder shaping:
   ◆ BO first 7 (8, 9, 9) sts. Finish row. Turn work.
   ◆ Work across row. Turn work.
   ◆ BO 7 (8, 9, 10) sts. Finish row. Turn work.
   ◆ Work across row. Turn work.
   ◆ BO last 8 (9, 9, 10) sts.

5. Complete neck shaping on left half of front:
   ◆ Sl sts from stitch holder back onto needle.
   ◆ Leaving center 2 sts on a safety pin, join yarn at neck edge and complete shaping as for right front.

6. Cont until work measures 23 (25, 27, 29)" from bottom.

7. Work left shoulder the same as right shoulder, but reverse shaping.

SLEEVES

1. With #6 needles and red yarns, CO 36 (40, 44, 48) sts. Work in K1, P1 rib for about 1½", following striping sequence.
   ◆ Inc 4 sts evenly across last row of rib [40 (44, 48, 52) sts].

2. Switch to #8 needles. Work in seed st, following color sequence.
   ◆ Inc 1 st at each end every 6 (6, 6, 7) rows 17 times [74 (78, 82, 86) sts; 17 (18, 19, 20)" wide].

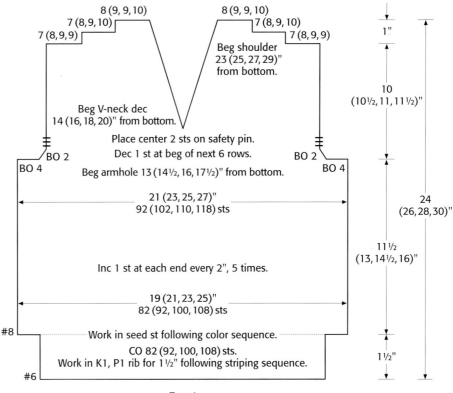

Dec 1 st at neck edges:
 Small: every 6 rows 7 times, then every 4 rows 7 times.
 Medium: every 4 rows 16 times.
 Large: every 4 rows 18 times.
 X-large: every 4 rows 15 times, then every 2 rows 5 times.

8 (9, 9, 10)   8 (9, 9, 10)
7 (8,9,10)   7 (8,9,10)
7 (8,9,9)   7 (8,9,9)

Beg shoulder
23 (25, 27, 29)"
from bottom.

1"

Beg V-neck dec
14 (16, 18, 20)" from bottom.

Place center 2 sts on safety pin.
Dec 1 st at beg of next 6 rows.
Beg armhole 13 (14½, 16, 17½)" from bottom.

BO 2   BO 2
BO 4   BO 4

10
(10½, 11, 11½)"

21 (23, 25, 27)"
92 (102, 110, 118) sts

24
(26, 28, 30)"

Inc 1 st at each end every 2", 5 times.

11½
(13, 14½, 16)"

19 (21, 23, 25)"
82 (92, 100, 108) sts

#8   Work in seed st following color sequence.

CO 82 (92, 100, 108) sts.
Work in K1, P1 rib for 1½" following striping sequence.

#6

1½"

Front

3. Cont until work measures 18 (19, 20, 21)" from bottom.

4. Beg cap shaping:
   - BO 4 sts at beg of next 2 rows.
   - BO 2 sts at beg of next 2 rows.
   - Dec 1 st at beg of next 8 (4, 0, 0) rows.
   - BO 2 sts at beg of next 18 (22, 26, 28) rows.
   - BO last 18 sts.

FINISHING

1. Sew shoulder seams.

2. V-neck rib: With #5 circular needle and RS facing, pick up a total of 132 (136, 140, 144) sts, beg at left shoulder:
   - Pick up 50 sts from shoulder to center of V.
   - Knit the 2 sts on safety pin (leaving the pin for identification).
   - Pick up 50 sts from 2 marked sts to right shoulder.

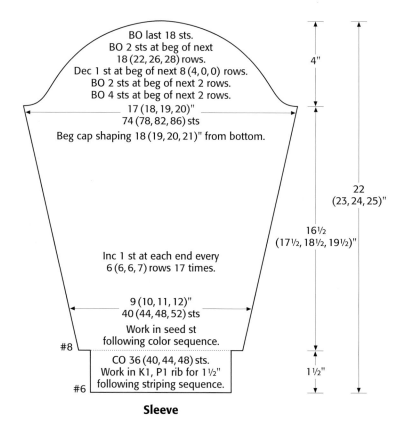

Sleeve

- Pick up 30 (34, 38, 42) sts from shoulder to shoulder.

3. Work in K2, P2 rib, following striping pattern to last st before marked sts at V:
   - With this last st and first of 2 marked sts, K2tog.
   - Sl 2nd marked st (as to knit) to right-hand needle and knit following st.
   - Now PSSO and cont in rib pattern, matching the opposite side.

4. Rep this dec EOR, remembering to always keep the center 2 marked sts as knit sts. BO on 12th (RS) row.

5. Sew in sleeves. Sew side and sleeve seams.

6. Block sweater to desired measurements.

7. Stabilize back neck and shoulders.

TIP

When working with slippery yarns that tend to "self-destruct" into knotted messes, place each skein into its own zippered sandwich bag. Cut a very small notch in one corner, just big enough for the yarn to run through.

THE SAMPLER SWEATER

For new knitters, one of the most exciting, yet at the same time intimidating, prospects is knitting a sweater in a pattern stitch. The idea behind this sweater was to take a classic yarn, explore a variety of stitches—none of which requires a particular multiple—and combine them into a sampler of sorts that is fun to knit and easy for either men or women to wear. The selection of a 50% silk/50% cashmere yarn made this a truly enjoyable journey, and the combination of very simple stitches creates a sweater that appears more complex than it is to knit.

SIZES

Small (Medium, Large, X-Large)

Finished Chest: 42 (46, 50, 54)"

Finished Length: 24 (26, 28, 30)"

MATERIALS

Use a yarn that knits at 4.25 sts to 1".

16 (17, 18, 20) skeins of Filatura di Crosa Silky
   Cashmere, 49% cashmere and 51% silk,
   each approximately 82 yds [1312 (1394,
   1476, 1640) yds total]

#7 and #8 needles

#7 circular needle (24")

GAUGE

17 sts and 28 rows = 4" in pattern stitch on
   #8 needles

Always check gauge before starting sweater.
   Increase or decrease needle size to obtain
   correct gauge.

PATTERN 1: Seed Stitch

Row 1: *K1, P1*; rep from * to *.

Row 2: Purl the knit sts and knit the purl sts
   as they face you.

Rep rows 1 and 2.

PATTERN 2: Diagonal Rib Stitch

Row 1: *K2, P2*; rep from * to *.

Rows 2, 4, 6, 8: Work sts as they face you.

Row 3: K1, *P2, K2*; rep from * to *.

Row 5: *P2, K2*; rep from * to *.

Row 7: P1, *K2, P2*; rep from * to *.

Rep rows 1–8.

PATTERN 3: Roman Rib Stitch

Row 1: Knit.

Row 2: Purl.

Row 3: *K1, P1*; rep from * to *.

Row 4: Work sts as they face you.

Row 5: Knit.

Row 6: Purl.

Row 7: *K1, P1*; rep from * to *.

Row 8: Work sts as they face you.

Rep rows 1–8.

PATTERN 4: Oblique Stitch

Row 1: *K3, P1*; rep from * to *.

Rows 2, 4, 6, 8: Work sts as they face you.

Row 3: *P1, K3*; rep from * to *.

Row 5: K1, *P1, K3*; rep from * to *.

Row 7: K2, *P1, K3*; rep from * to *.

Rep rows 1–8.

PATTERN 5: Mock Rib

Row 1: *K1, P1*; rep from * to *.

Row 2: Purl.

Rep rows 1 and 2.

PATTERN 6: Raised Separating Bar Pattern

Row 1: Knit.

Rows 2 and 3: Purl.

Rows 4 and 5: Knit.

Row 6: Purl.

Rep rows 1–6.

BACK

1. With #7 needles, CO 82 (90, 98, 106) sts. Work K1, P1 rib for 2". End with WS row.

2. With RS facing and #8 needles, work pattern 6.

3. Inc 1 st at each end every 2" 4 times while working in patterns as follows:
   ◆ Work in pattern 1 for 3½ (4, 4½, 5)".
   ◆ Work pattern 6.
   ◆ Work in pattern 2 for 3½ (4, 4½, 5)".
   ◆ Work pattern 6.
   ◆ Work in pattern 3 for 3½ (4, 4½, 5)".
   [90 (98, 106, 114) sts; 21 (23, 25, 27)" wide].

4. When work measures 13 (14½, 16, 17½)", beg armhole shaping, staying in pattern stitch:
   ◆ BO 4 sts at beg of next 2 rows.
   ◆ BO 3 sts at beg of next 2 rows.
   ◆ BO 2 sts at beg of next 2 rows.
   ◆ Dec 1 st at beg of next 4 rows [68 (76, 84, 92) sts; 16 (18, 20, 22)" wide].

5. Rep pattern 6.

6. Work in pattern 4 for 3½ (4, 4½, 5)".

7. Rep pattern 6.

8. Work in pattern 5 until work measures 23 (25, 27, 29)" from bottom.

9. Beg back neck and shoulder shaping:
   ◆ BO first 6 (7, 8, 9) sts. Work next 13 (15, 17, 18) sts. Keeping 14 (16, 18, 19) sts on right-hand needle, BO center 28 (30, 32, 36) sts. Finish row. Turn work.
   ◆ BO first 6 (7, 8, 9) sts. Finish row to neck edge. Turn work.
   ◆ Dec 1 st at neck edge. Finish row. Turn work.
   ◆ BO 6 (7, 8, 9) sts. Finish row. Turn work.
   ◆ Work across row. Turn work.
   ◆ BO last 7 (8, 9, 9) sts.

10. Complete back neck and shoulder shaping:
    ◆ Join yarn at neck edge. Dec 1 st and finish row. Turn work.
    ◆ BO 6 (7, 8, 9) sts. Finish row. Turn work.
    ◆ Work across row. Turn work.
    ◆ BO last 7 (8, 9, 9) sts.

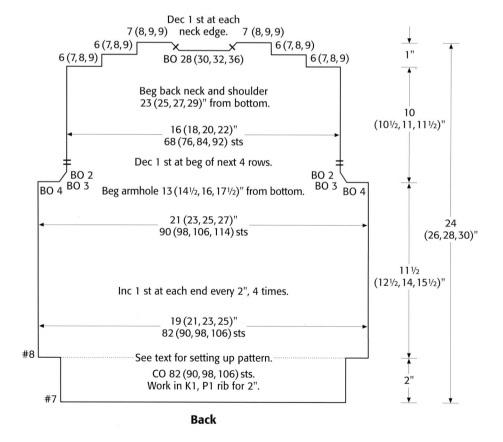

Back

FRONT

1. Work front exactly the same as back until work measures 21 (23, 25, 27)" from bottom.

2. Beg front neck shaping:
   ◆ Work first 28 (31, 34, 36) sts. BO center 12 (14, 16, 20) sts. Finish row. Turn work.
   ◆ Work across row. Turn work.
   ◆ BO 3 sts at neck edge. Finish row. Turn work.
   ◆ Work across row. Turn work.
   ◆ BO 2 sts at neck edge EOR 2 times.
   ◆ Dec 1 st at neck edge EOR 2 times.

3. Cont in pattern stitch until work measures 23 (25, 27, 29)" from bottom.

4. Beg shoulder shaping:
   ◆ BO 6 (7, 8, 9) sts at outside edge. Finish row. Turn work.
   ◆ Work across row. Turn work.
   ◆ BO 6 (7, 8, 9) sts. Finish row. Turn work.
   ◆ Work across the row. Turn work.
   ◆ BO last 7 (8, 9, 9) sts.

5. Complete front neck shaping:
   ◆ Join yarn at neck edge. BO 3 sts at neck edge and finish row. Turn work.
   ◆ Work across row. Turn work.
   ◆ BO 2 sts at neck edge EOR 2 times.
   ◆ Dec 1 st at neck edge EOR 2 times.

6. Cont in pattern stitch until work measures 23 (25, 27, 29)" from bottom.

7. Complete shoulder shaping as in step 4 above.

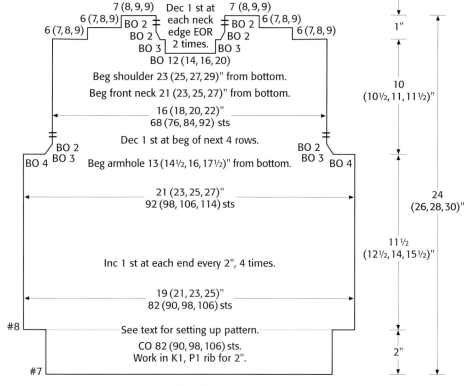

Front

SLEEVES

1. With #7 needles, CO 34 (40, 44, 48) sts. Work K1, P1 rib for 2½". Inc 4 sts evenly in last row of rib. End with WS row [38 (44, 48, 52) sts].

2. With RS facing and #8 needles, work pattern 6.

3. Inc 1 st at each end every 4 (5, 5, 5) rows 18 (17, 17, 17) times, working in pattern(s) as follows:
   - Work in pattern 1 for 4 (4½, 4²/₃, 5)".
   - Work pattern 6.
   - Work in pattern 2 for 4 (4½, 4²/₃, 5)".
   - Work pattern 6.
   - Work in pattern 3 for 4 (4½, 4²/₃, 5)" [74 (78, 82, 86) sts; 17 (18, 19, 20)" wide].

4. At the same time, when work measures 16 (17, 18, 19)" from bottom, beg armhole shaping. (Staying in pattern while binding off is trickier than you might think. The key is to concentrate. Good luck!)
   - BO 4 sts at beg of next 2 rows.
   - BO 3 sts at beg of next 2 rows.
   - Dec 1 st at beg of next 12 rows.
   - BO 2 sts at beg of next 18 rows.
   - BO last 12 (16, 20, 24) sts.

FINISHING

1. Sew shoulder seams.

2. Pick up a total of 82 (82, 86, 90) sts:
   - Pick up 37 (37, 39, 41) sts across back neck from shoulder to shoulder.
   - Pick up 45 (45, 47, 49) sts across front neck from shoulder to shoulder.

3. Work in K1, P1 rib for 1". BO loosely.

4. Sew in sleeves. Sew side and sleeve seams.

5. Block sweater to desired measurements.

6. Stabilize back neck and shoulders.

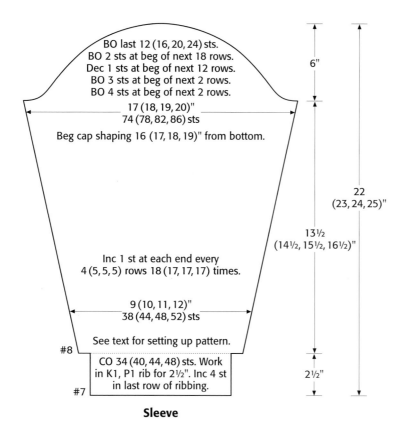

BO last 12 (16, 20, 24) sts.
BO 2 sts at beg of next 18 rows.
Dec 1 sts at beg of next 12 rows.
BO 3 sts at beg of next 2 rows.
BO 4 sts at beg of next 2 rows.

17 (18, 19, 20)"
74 (78, 82, 86) sts

Beg cap shaping 16 (17, 18, 19)" from bottom.

6"

22 (23, 24, 25)"

13½ (14½, 15½, 16½)"

Inc 1 st at each end every 4 (5, 5, 5) rows 18 (17, 17, 17) times.

9 (10, 11, 12)"
38 (44, 48, 52) sts

See text for setting up pattern.

#8

CO 34 (40, 44, 48) sts. Work in K1, P1 rib for 2½". Inc 4 st in last row of ribbing.

#7

2½"

Sleeve

TIP

When working on multiple patterns in a sweater, it is always a good idea to actually count the number of rows worked in each pattern to help ensure that the front and back and both sleeves line up correctly when the pieces are finished.

DR. SAM'S VEST

Dr. Sam found Tricoter while he was still in medical school at the University of Washington. His father had driven by Tricoter and seen men's sweaters in our windows. Knowing that his son loved hand-knit sweaters, he told Dr. Sam about our store. Sam stopped in, thinking he would purchase a sweater, not realizing that we were primarily a yarn shop and what he had seen were our newest samples. This piqued his creative side and before long, Sam had not only learned to knit, but was designing his own sweaters. He often took his knitting to the hospital to help keep him awake during long shifts "on call" throughout his residency! Dr. Sam even became the teacher for our Beginning Knitting classes on his weekends off and developed a very loyal group of knitters. Sam has moved on to practice sports medicine and rehabilitation in the Denver area now, but we stay in touch. It is with pride and gratitude that we include one of Sam's first sweater designs. We look forward to new designs with Sam's visits.

SIZES

Small (Medium, Large, X-Large)
Finished Chest: 42 (46, 50, 54)"
Finished Length: 24 (26, 28, 30)"

MATERIALS

Use a yarn that knits at 5 sts to 1".
6 (7, 7, 8) skeins of On Line Clipp, 100%
    Egyptian cotton, each approximately 181
    yds [1086 (1267, 1267, 1448) yds total]
#4 and #6 needles
5 (5, 6, 6) buttons, approximately ¾" in
    diameter
Stitch holders

GAUGE

20 sts and 32 rows = 4" in garter st on #6
    needles
Always check gauge before starting sweater.
    Increase or decrease needle size to obtain
    correct gauge.

> ### TIP
>
> It is very important to check your gauge when working in garter stitch. Go down a needle size if necessary to ensure firm tension. This will help to give a uniform appearance to your work and avoid the tendency of garter-stitch garments to "grow" in length.

BACK

1. With #4 needles, CO 94 (104, 114,
    124) sts. Work in garter st for 1".

2. Switch to #6 needles. Cont in garter
    st, inc 1 st at each end every 20 (22,
    24, 26) rows 6 times [106 (116, 126,
    136) sts; 21 (23, 25, 27)" wide].

3. Cont until work measures 14 (15½,
    17, 18½)" from bottom.

4. Beg armhole shaping:
    ◆ BO 5 sts at beg of next 2 rows.
    ◆ BO 3 sts at beg of next 2 rows.
    ◆ BO 2 sts at beg of next 4 rows.

◆ Dec 1 st at beg of next 2 rows
[80 (90, 100, 110) sts; 16 (18, 20,
22)" wide].

5. Cont in garter st until work measures
    23 (25, 27, 29)" from bottom.

6. Beg back neck and shoulder shaping:
    ◆ BO first 7 (8, 9, 11) sts. Knit next
    14 (17, 20, 22) sts. Keeping 15 (18,
    21, 23) sts on right-hand needle, BO
    center 36 (38, 40, 42) sts. Finish
    row. Turn work.
    ◆ BO first 7 (8, 9, 11) sts. Finish
    row. Turn work.

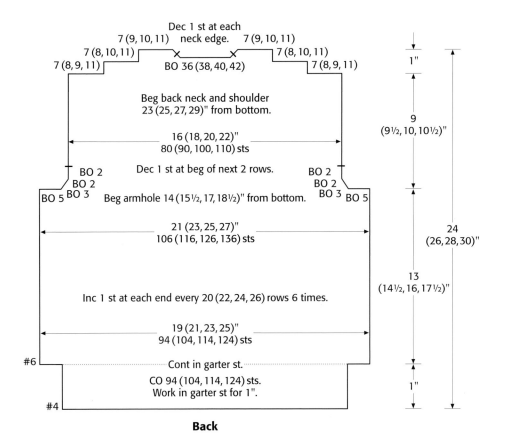

Back

- Dec 1 st at neck edge. Finish row. Turn work.
- BO first 7 (8, 10, 11) sts. Finish row. Turn work.
- Knit across row. Turn work.
- BO last 7 (9, 10, 11) sts.

7. Complete back neck and shoulder shaping:
   - Join yarn at neck edge. Dec 1 st and finish row. Turn work.
   - BO first 7 (8, 10, 11) sts. Finish row. Turn work.
   - Knit across row. Turn work.
   - BO last 7 (9, 10, 11) sts.

FRONTS

1. With #4 needles, CO 54 (58, 64, 69) sts. Work in garter st for 1". Work right and left fronts (refers to your right and left sides), beg with right front.

2. Switch to #6 needles. Cont in garter st, inc 1 st at outside edge every 20 (22, 24, 26) rows 6 times [60 (64, 70, 75) sts; 12 (13, 14, 15)" wide].

3. Cont in garter st until work measures 14 (15½, 17, 18½)" from bottom.

4. Beg armhole shaping:
   - BO 5 sts at outside edge.
   - BO 3 sts at outside edge.
   - BO 2 sts at outside edge EOR 2 times.
   - Dec 1 st at outside edge [47 (51, 57, 62) sts; 9 (10, 11, 12)" wide].

5. Cont until work measures 21 (23, 25, 27)" from bottom.

6. Beg front neck shaping:
   - Beg at neck edge, place first 17 (17, 19, 20) sts on a holder. Finish row. Turn work.
   - Knit across row. Turn work.
   - BO 4 sts at neck edge. Finish row. Turn work.
   - Knit across row. Turn work.
   - BO 2 sts at neck edge. Finish row. Turn work.
   - Dec 1 st at neck edge EOR 3 times.

7. Cont in garter st until work measures 23 (25, 27, 29)" from bottom.

8. Beg shoulder shaping:
   - Starting at outside edge, BO 7 (8, 9, 11) sts. Finish row. Turn work.
   - Knit across row. Turn work.
   - BO 7 (8, 10, 11) sts. Finish row. Turn work.
   - Knit across row. Turn work.
   - BO last 7 (9, 10, 11) sts.

9. Mark placement for buttons on right front.

10. Work left front the same as right front, but reverse shaping. Work 5 (5, 6, 6) three-stitch horizontal buttonholes, placed 3 sts in from

7 (9, 10, 11)
7 (8, 10, 11)
7 (8, 9, 11)
Dec 1 st at neck edge EOR 3 times.
BO 2
BO 4
BO 17 (17, 19, 20)
Beg shoulder 23 (25, 27, 29)" from bottom.
Beg front neck 21 (23, 25, 27)" from bottom.
9 (10, 11, 12)"
47 (51, 57, 62) sts
Dec 1 st at outside edge.
BO 2
BO 2
BO 5 BO 3
12 (13, 14, 15)"
60 (64, 70, 75) sts
Beg armhole 14 (15½, 17, 18½)" from bottom.
1"
9 (9½, 10, 10½)"
24 (26, 28, 30)"
13 (14½, 16, 17½)"
Inc 1 st at outside edge every 20 (22, 24, 26) rows 6 times.
Note: on left front, work 5 (5, 6, 6) three-stitch horizontal buttonholes, placed 3 sts in from front edge.
11 (12, 13, 14)"
54 (58, 64, 69) sts
#6 Cont in garter st.
CO 54 (58, 64, 69) sts. Work in garter st for 1".
1"
#4

Front

front edge. Space buttonholes to line up with button placement on right front.

FINISHING

1. Sew shoulder seams.

2. Neckband: With RS facing and #4 needles, pick up a total of 96 (98, 102, 108) sts:
   - Pick up 30 (30, 31, 33) sts from right front—including 17 (17, 19, 20) sts from holder—to right shoulder.
   - Pick up 36 (38, 40, 42) sts from shoulder to shoulder across back neck.
   - Pick up 30 (30, 31, 33) sts from left shoulder—including 17 (17, 19, 20) sts from holder—to left front.
   - Work in garter st for 2 more rows.
   - BO loosely on 4th row.

3. Knit armhole bands before sewing side seams so you can use straight needles. With RS facing and #4 needles, pick up 104 (110, 116, 122) sts:
   - Work 2 more rows in garter st.
   - BO loosely on 4th row.

4. Sew side seams.

5. Block vest to desired measurements.

6. Stabilize back neck and shoulders.

TIP

Practice making buttonholes on a swatch before knitting them into your work to get a more professional appearance.

EX LIBRIS

"When you reread a classic you do not see more in the book than you did before; you see more in you than there was before." —CLIFTON FADIMAN

It has been said that every modern idea is really the reinterpretation of a concept that has already been expressed. That well may be true, but our appreciation for classics—books, cars, architecture, etc.—is proof that when the original is good, the versions that it inspires get better and better. The sweaters in this section are all our original designs but have elements that were taken from some of our favorite classic sweaters over the years.

LARRY'S IRISH VEST

t was on a trip to Ireland to mark a major birthday and fulfill a lifelong dream to investigate his Celtic roots that Beryl's fiancé, Larry, discovered a passion for the Irish manner of haberdashery. This vest that Beryl designed for him incorporates a rich complexity of colors and textures and follows the traditional style of tailored menswear vests, with a solid back and patterned fronts, translated in rich jewel-toned cashmeres and wool. We've found that women, too, love this classic style.

SIZES

Small (Medium, Large, X-Large)

Finished Chest: 40 (44, 48, 52)"

Finished Length: 22 (23, 24, 25)"

MATERIALS

For back: Use a yarn that knits at 4.75 sts to 1" on #6 needles in St st.

For fronts: Use a combination of yarns that knit at 5.5 sts to 1" on #7 needles.

3 (3, 4, 4) skeins of Multi-Tweed Noro Menou, 55% wool, 15% silk, and 30% cotton, (MC), each approximately 132 yds [396 (396, 525, 525) yds total]

7 (7, 8, 8) total skeins of Filatura di Crosa, 100% cashmere, each approximately 153 yds [1070 (1070, 1224, 1224) yds total], in the following colors:

A	4 (4, 5, 5) skeins	Black, color #002
B	1 skein	Hunter, color #50
C	1 skein	Purple, color #1875
D	1 skein	Olive, color #1872

#5, #6, and #7 needles

#5 circular needle (29")

6 buttons, approximately ½" in diameter

GAUGE

For back: 19 sts and 28 rows = 4" in pattern stitch on #6 needles

For fronts: 22 sts and 25 rows = 4" in pattern stitch on #7 needles

Always check gauge before starting sweater. Increase or decrease needle size to obtain correct gauge.

STRIPING PATTERN (for rib)

Cast on: A

Row 1: D

Row 2: MC

Row 3: C

Row 4: MC

Row 5: B

Row 6: MC

Row 7: A

DIAMOND BROCADE STITCH (for back)

(multiple of 8 sts, plus 1)

Row 1 (RS): K1 (edge st), K3, *P1, K7*; rep from * to *, end P1, K3, K1 (edge st).

Row 2: P3, *K1, P1, K1, P5*; rep from * to *, end P3.

Row 3: K2, *P1, K3*; rep from * to *, end K2.

Row 4: P1, *K1, P5, K1, P1*; rep from * to *.

Row 5: *P1, K7*; rep from * to *, end P1.

Row 6: Rep row 4.

Row 7: Rep row 3.

Row 8: Rep row 2.

Rep rows 1–8.

DOTTED STRIPES STITCH (for fronts)

(multiple of 3 sts, plus 2)

Row 1 (RS): With MC, knit (includes 2 edge sts).

Row 2: With MC, *P2, K1*; rep from * to *, end P2.

Row 3: *K2 with MC, K1 with A*; rep from * to *, end K2 with MC.

Row 4: *P2 with MC, K1 with A*; rep from * to *, end P2 with MC.

Rows 5–6: Rep rows 1–2.

Rows 7–8: Rep rows 3–4 with B instead of A.

Rows 9–10: Rep rows 1–2.

Rows 11–12: Rep rows 3–4 with A.

Rows 13–14: Rep rows 1–2.

Rows 15–16: Rep rows 3–4 with C instead of A.

Rows 17–18: Rep rows 1–2.

Rows 19–20: Rep rows 3–4 with A.

Rows 21–22: Rep rows 1–2.

Rows 23–24: Rep rows 3–4 with D instead of A.

Repeat rows 1–24.

BACK

1. With #5 needles and color A, CO 98 (106, 114, 122) sts. Work in K1, P1 rib for 1", following striping pattern. Inc 1 st in last row of rib [99 (107, 115, 123) sts].

2. With RS facing, #6 needles, and color A, set up Diamond Brocade stitch: K5, *P1, K7*; rep from * to *, end P1, K5.

3. Cont in Diamond Brocade stitch until work measures 11 (11½, 12, 12)" from bottom [20 (22, 24, 26)" wide].

4. Beg armhole shaping (in pattern):
   - BO 4 sts at beg of next 6 rows.
   - BO 2 sts at beg of next 2 rows.

   - Dec 1 st at beg of next 12 rows. [59 (67, 75, 83) sts; 12½ (14, 15½, 17½)" wide].

5. Cont until work measures 21 (22, 23, 24)" from bottom.

6. Beg back neck and shoulder shaping:
   - BO first 4 (5, 6, 7) sts. Knit next 9 (11, 13, 15) sts. Keeping 10 (12, 14, 16) sts on right-hand needle, BO center 32 (34, 36, 38) sts. Finish row. Turn work.
   - BO first 4 (5, 6, 7) sts. Finish row. Turn work.
   - Dec 1 st at neck edge. Finish row. Turn work.
   - BO 4 (5, 6, 7) sts. Finish row. Turn work.
   - Work across row. Turn work.
   - BO last 5 (6, 7, 8) sts.

7. Complete back neck and shoulder shaping:
   - Join yarn at neck edge. Dec 1 st and finish row. Turn work.
   - BO 4 (5, 6, 7) sts. Finish row. Turn work.
   - Work across row. Turn work.
   - BO last 5 (6, 7, 8) sts.

FRONTS

1. With #5 needles and color A, CO 55 (58, 61, 67) sts. Work in K1, P1 rib for 1", following striping pattern.

2. With RS facing and #7 needles, switch to MC and beg Dotted Stripes stitch.

3. Cont in Dotted Stripes stitch until work measures 11 (11½, 12, 12)" from bottom.

4. Beg armhole shaping:
   - BO 4 sts at outside edge. Finish row. Turn work.
   - Work across row. Turn work.
   - BO 3 sts at outside edge. Finish row. Turn work.
   - Work across row. Turn work.
   - BO 2 sts at outside edge EOR 3 times.
   - Dec 1 st at outside edge EOR 4 times.

5. At 12 (13, 14, 15)" from bottom, beg V-neck shaping (while cont armhole shaping):
   - Dec 1 st at neck edge.

Dec 1 st at each neck edge.
5 (6, 7, 8)   5 (6, 7, 8)
4 (5, 6, 7)   4 (5, 6, 7)
4 (5, 6, 7)   BO 32 (34, 36, 38)   4 (5, 6, 7)

Beg back neck and shoulder 21 (22, 23, 24)" from bottom.

12½ (14, 15½, 17½)"
59 (67, 75, 83) sts
Dec 1 st at beg of next 12 rows.

1"

10 (10½, 11, 12)"

BO 2
BO 4
BO 4 BO 4   BO 2
              BO 4
              BO 4 BO 4

Beg armhole 11 (11½, 12, 12)" from bottom.

22 (23, 24, 25)"

20 (22, 24, 26)"
99 (107, 115, 123) sts

10 (10½, 11, 11)"

#6

See text for setting up pattern.
CO 98 (106, 114, 122) sts. Work in K1, P1 rib for 1" following striping pattern. Inc 1 st in last row of ribbing.

1"

#5

Back

For small and medium: every 4 rows 8 times, then EOR 14 times. **For large and X-large:** EOR 25 times.

6. Cont until work measures 21 (22, 23, 24)" from bottom.

7. Complete shoulder shaping:
   - BO first 5 (6, 6, 8) sts at outside edge. Finish row. Turn work.
   - Work across row. Turn work.
   - BO 5 (6, 6, 8) sts. Finish row. Turn work.
   - Work across row. Turn work.
   - BO last 6 (7, 7, 9) sts.

8. Work second front the same as first front, but reverse shaping.

FINISHING

1. Sew shoulder seams. You will have a different number of sts at the shoulder on the back than you will on the fronts. This is because the yarns are different gauges. The sizes of the actual pieces should be approximately the same width to allow neat seams that match when sewn together.

2. Front bands: With RS facing and a #5 circular needle, pick up a total of 280 (286, 292, 298) sts in striping sequence:
   - Pick up 66 (68, 70, 72) sts from lower right front to first V-neck dec.
   - Pick up 58 sts from beg of the V-neck to shoulder seam.
   - Pick up 32 (34, 36, 38) sts from shoulder seam to shoulder seam.
   - Pick up 58 sts from shoulder seam to beg of V-neck.
   - Pick up 66 (68, 70, 72) sts from beg of V-neck to lower left front.

3. Work in K1, P1 rib for 6 rows. On buttonhole side, work 6 buttonholes in the 4th row of rib, spacing them evenly between the bottom and first neck dec. BO.

4. Armhole bands: With RS facing and a #5 circular needle, pick up 120 (124, 128, 134) sts, following striping sequence:
   - Work in K1, P1 rib for 6 rows. BO.

5. Sew side seams.

6. Sew on buttons to correspond with buttonholes.

7. Block vest to desired measurements.

8. Stabilize back neck.

Front

HANS'S COMMUNITY PROJECT VEST

Hans is one of the true secrets of Tricoter's success! He owns and runs the espresso shop in our small complex and takes care of us throughout the day. When our business is really hectic and there is no time to run next door for a latte, Hans delivers! He know the names of all our customers, just how they like their coffee, and on what days they regularly come in to knit. He is always interested in what customers are knitting, checking on their progress when they stop in for a latte. It was at the suggestion of one of our customers that we began Hans's "Community Project Vest" one spring. We left out the basket of yarn and pattern, and each customer who came into the store and had a few extra minutes worked on it. One of the best features of the vest is the little irregularity here and there that is a "signature" of one of the knitters. The vest was our combined gift of love to Hans several years ago. We asked to borrow it to include in our book as it, like Hans, has become one of our favorites!

While all of the yarns in this vest have long been discontinued (in fact the Missoni name no longer exists in hand knitting yarns), we felt it was important enough to include. Beautiful new novelty yarns are introduced each year in this very common size. The fun with this kind of project is in creating your own unique combination of colors and textures.

SIZES

Small (Medium, Large, X-Large)
Finished Chest: 42 (46, 50, 54)"
Finished Length: 24 (26, 28, 30)"

MATERIALS

Use a yarn that knits at 4.0 sts to 1" on #8
needles.

8 (8, 8, 10) total skeins of Missoni Tweed (discontinued), each approximately 100 yds
[800 (800, 800, 1000) yards total], in the
following colors:

A	2 (2, 2, 3) skeins	Charcoal tweed
B	2 skeins	Gray tweed
C	2 (2, 2, 3) skeins	Blue tweed
D	2 skeins	Rust tweed

9 (9, 9, 10) total skeins of Missoni Giglio
(discontinued), each approximately 100 yds
[900 (900, 900, 1000) yds total] in the
following colors:

E	3 (3, 3, 4) skeins	Black
F	2 skeins	Plum

G	2 skeins	Teal
H	2 skeins	Gold

#6 and #8 needles
#6 circular needle (24")
Safety pin
Stitch holder

GAUGE

16 sts and 19 rows = 4" on #8 needle
Always check gauge before starting sweater.
  Increase or decrease needle size to obtain
  correct gauge.

STRIPING PATTERN (for rib)

Cast on: E
Row 1: G
Row 2: E
Row 3: F
Row 4: E
Row 5: H
Rep rows 1–5.

COLOR-WORK PATTERN

Rows 1–3: A
Row 4: G
Rows 5–7: A
Row 8: F
Row 9: E
Rows 10–11: E and H *1 st black, 2 sts gold*;
  rep from * to * (color work).
Row 12: E
Row 13: F
Rows 14–16: B
Row 17: G
Rows 18–20: A
Row 21: G
Rows 22–24: B

Row 25: F
Row 26: E
Rows 27–28: E and H *1 st black, 2 sts gold*;
  rep from * to * (color work).
Row 29: E
Row 30: F
Rows 31–33: C
Row 34: G
Rows 35–37: C
Row 38: F
Row 39: E
Rows 40–41: E and H *1 st black, 2 sts gold*;
  rep from * to * (color work).
Row 42: E
Row 43: F
Rows 44–46: D
Row 47: G
Rows 48–50: C
Row 51: G
Rows 52–54: D
Row 55: F
Row 56: E
Rows 57–58: E and H *1 st black, 2 sts gold*;
  rep from * to * (color work).
Row 59: E
Row 60: F
Rep these 60 rows.

BACK

1. With #6 needles, CO 86 (94, 102,
   110) sts. Work in K1, P1 rib for 2½",
   following striping pattern. Work
   through sequence twice plus 1 more
   row in black.

2. Switch to #8 needles and work in
   color pattern in St st until work

measures 13 (14½, 16, 17)" from bottom [21 (23, 25, 27)" wide].

3. Beg armhole shaping:
   - BO 5 sts at beg of next 2 rows.
   - BO 3 sts at beg of next 2 rows.
   - BO 2 sts at beg of next 2 rows.
   - Dec 1 st at beg of next 4 rows. [62 (70, 78, 86) sts; 15 (17, 19, 21)" wide].

4. Cont in color-work pattern until work measures 23 (25, 27, 29)" from bottom.

5. Beg back neck and shoulder shaping:
   - BO first 5 (6, 7, 8) sts. Knit the next 13 (15, 17, 19) sts. Keeping 14 (16, 18, 20) sts on right-hand needle,

BO center 26 (28, 30, 32) sts. Finish row. Turn work.
   - BO 5 (6, 7, 8) sts. Finish row. Turn work.
   - Dec 1 st at neck edge. Finish row. Turn work.
   - BO 6 (7, 8, 9) sts. Finish row. Turn work.
   - Work across row. Turn work.
   - BO last 6 (7, 8, 9) sts.

6. Complete back neck and shoulder shaping:
   - Join yarn at neck edge. Dec 1 st and finish row. Turn work.
   - BO 6 (7, 8, 9) sts. Finish row.

Turn work.
   - Work across row. Turn work.
   - BO last 6 (7, 8, 9) sts.

FRONT

1. Work rib as for back but inc 1 st in last row of rib. Cont as for back until work measures 13 (14½, 16, 17)" from bottom [87 (95, 103, 111) sts; 21 (23, 25, 27)" wide].

2. Beg V-neck shaping, working right front first (see directions for decrease on page 131): Sl first 43 (47, 51, 55) sts onto a stitch holder. Place a safety pin in next (center) st and finish row. Turn work.
   - Dec 1 st at neck edge alternating every 2nd and 4th row 14 (15, 16, 17) times [17 (20, 23, 26) sts].

3. Cont in color-work pattern until work measures 23 (25, 27, 29)" from bottom.

4. Complete shoulder shaping:
   - BO first 5 (6, 7, 8) sts at outside edge. Finish row. Turn work.
   - Work across row. Turn work.
   - BO 6 (7, 8, 9) sts. Finish row. Turn work.
   - Work across row. Turn work.
   - BO last 6 (7, 8, 9) sts.

5. Join yarn at center front, keeping center st on stitch marker. Work left front the same as right front, but reverse shaping.

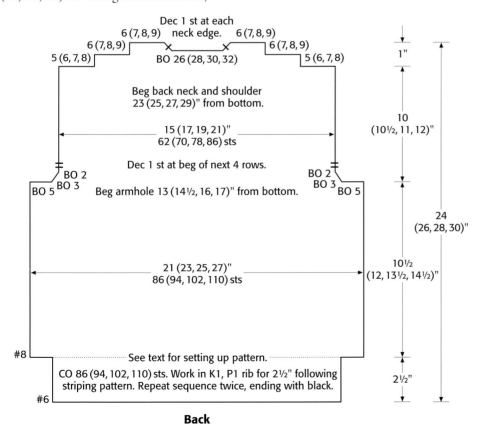

Dec 1 st at each neck edge.

6 (7, 8, 9)   6 (7, 8, 9)   6 (7, 8, 9)   6 (7, 8, 9)
5 (6, 7, 8)   BO 26 (28, 30, 32)   5 (6, 7, 8)

1"

Beg back neck and shoulder 23 (25, 27, 29)" from bottom.

15 (17, 19, 21)"
62 (70, 78, 86) sts

10 (10½, 11, 12)"

Dec 1 st at beg of next 4 rows.

BO 2   BO 2
BO 5 BO 3   Beg armhole 13 (14½, 16, 17)" from bottom.   BO 3 BO 5

24 (26, 28, 30)"

21 (23, 25, 27)"
86 (94, 102, 110) sts

10½ (12, 13½, 14½)"

#8   See text for setting up pattern.
CO 86 (94, 102, 110) sts. Work in K1, P1 rib for 2½" following striping pattern. Repeat sequence twice, ending with black.
#6

2½"

Back

FINISHING

1. Sew shoulder seams.

2. Work front V-neck rib, following striping pattern: With RS facing and #6 circular needle, pick up a total of 124 (130, 136, 146) sts:
   • Pick up 47 (49, 51, 55) sts from left shoulder to V-neck.
   • Knit center st, leaving safety pin in it.
   • Pick up 47 (49, 51, 55) sts from V-neck to right shoulder.
   • Pick up 29 (31, 33, 35) sts from shoulder to shoulder.
   • Work in rib pattern in striping sequence to last st before center st.

3. Complete neck rib:
   • Insert right-hand needle into center st and the one before it as if to K2tog, but instead, sl them onto right-hand needle.
   • Knit next st. Go back and sl 2 previous sts over this last st as one and cont in rib pattern, matching opposite side.
   • Work this dec on alternating rows.
   • On opposite rows, always knit center (marked) st.
   • Work through striping sequence once. BO with black.

4. Armhole bands: With #6 needles and RS facing, pick up 90 (94, 98, 106) sts, working through striping sequence once in K1, P1 rib. BO with black.

5. Sew side seams.

6. Block vest to desired measurements.

7. Stabilize back neck.

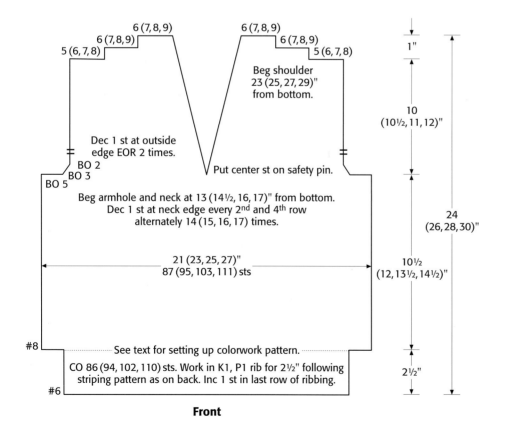

6 (7, 8, 9)

6 (7, 8, 9)   6 (7, 8, 9)

5 (6, 7, 8)   6 (7, 8, 9)

5 (6, 7, 8)

Beg shoulder
23 (25, 27, 29)"
from bottom.

1"

10
(10½, 11, 12)"

Dec 1 st at outside
edge EOR 2 times.
BO 2
BO 3
BO 5

Put center st on safety pin.

Beg armhole and neck at 13 (14½, 16, 17)" from bottom.
Dec 1 st at neck edge every 2nd and 4th row
alternately 14 (15, 16, 17) times.

24
(26, 28, 30)"

21 (23, 25, 27)"
87 (95, 103, 111) sts

10½
(12, 13½, 14½)"

#8

See text for setting up colorwork pattern.

CO 86 (94, 102, 110) sts. Work in K1, P1 rib for 2½" following
striping pattern as on back. Inc 1 st in last row of ribbing.

2½"

#6

Front

JAMES'S CABLED CASHMERE VEST

We have lost track of the number of sweaters and vests that we've knit for James, but we know that he has inspired some of our finest work. We had no idea when we met this handsome, charming, impeccably dressed man that his passion for beautiful fibers and attention to minute details would be the beginning of a wonderful friendship. This cashmere vest is representative of James's collection. He loved the complex look of the interwoven cables in a classic vest tailored enough to wear under a sportcoat yet interesting enough to wear without it. James's discerning eye for unique details has challenged our design skills more than once. He'll often come to us with a specific color, texture, or finishing technique for us to translate in his next sweater. We're certain that meeting James's expectations has made us better knitters!

SIZES

Small (Medium, Large, X-Large)

Finished Chest: 42 (46, 50, 54)"

Finished Length: 23 (25, 27, 29)"

MATERIALS

Use a yarn that knits at 5.2 sts to 1" in St st.

11 (12, 13, 14) skeins of Noro Cashmel,
100% cashmere, each approximately 105
yds [1155 (1260, 1365,1470) yds total]

#4 and #5 needles

Cable needle

Stitch holder

2 row counters

GAUGE

30 sts and 27 rows = 4" in cable pattern on
#5 needles

Always check gauge before starting sweater.
Increase or decrease needle size to obtain
correct gauge.

CABLE A (12-stitch cable)

Row 1 (RS): P1, K12, P1.

Row 2 (WS): K1, P12, K1.

Rows 3 and 4: Rep row 2.

Row 5: P1, C6F, P1.

Rows 6, 8, 10, 12, 16: Rep row 1.

Rows 7, 9, 11, 13, 15: Rep row 2.

Rep rows 5–16.

CABLE B (15-stitch cable)

Row 1 (RS): P1, K15, P1.

Row 2 (WS): K1, P15, K1.

Row 3: Rep row 1.

Row 4: Rep row 2.

Row 5: P1, K5, C5F, P1.

Rows 6, 8, 10, 12, 14: Rep row 2.

Rows 7, 9, 11, 13: Rep row 1.

Row 15: P1, C5B, K5, P1.

Rows 16, 18, 20, 22, 24: Rep row 2.

Rows 17, 19, 21, 23: Rep row 1.

Rep rows 5–24.

BACK

1. With #4 needles, CO 116 (126, 136, 146) sts. Work in K1, P1 rib for 2½", inc 46 (47, 55, 57) sts evenly across last row of rib. End with (WS) row [162 (173, 191, 203) sts].

2. Set up cable pattern (includes edge sts):

Small: K1, *K15, P1, K12, P1*; rep from * to * 4 times, end K16.

Medium: K7, P1, K12, P1, *K15, P1, K12, P1*; rep from * to * 4 times, end K7.

Large: K1, *K15, P1, K12, P1*; rep from * to * 5 times, end K16.

X-Large: K7, P1, *K15, P1, K12, P1*; rep from * to * 5 times, end K15, P1, K7.

3. Cont in pattern, remembering to work the first cable twist on both the 12- and 15-stitch cables on the 5th row. From this point, the 12-stitch

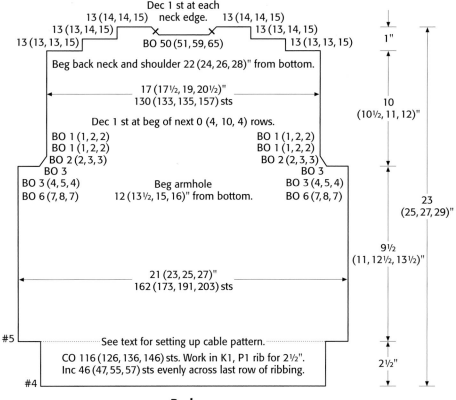

Back

cable will twist to the front on every 12th (RS) row, and the 15-stitch cable will alternately twist from left side to right side, every 10th (RS) row.

4. Cont in pattern until work measures 12 (13½, 15, 16)" from bottom [21 (23, 25, 27)" wide].

5. Beg armhole shaping:
   - BO 6 (7, 8, 7) sts at beg of next 2 rows.
   - BO 3 (4, 5, 4) sts at beg of next 2 rows.
   - BO 3 sts at beg of next 2 rows.
   - BO 2 (2, 3, 3) sts at beg of next 2 rows.
   - BO 1 (1, 2, 2) sts at beg of next 2 rows.
   - BO 1 (1, 2, 2) sts at beg of next 2 rows.
   - Dec 1 st at beg of next 0 (4, 10, 4) rows [130 (133, 135, 157) sts; 17 (17½, 19, 20½)" wide].

6. Cont in pattern until work measures 22 (24, 26, 28)" from bottom.

7. Beg back neck and shoulder shaping:
   - BO first 13 (13, 13, 15) sts. Work next 26 (27, 28, 30) sts. Keeping 27 (28, 29, 31) sts on right-hand needle, BO center 50 (51, 59, 65) sts. Finish row. Turn work.
   - BO first 13 (13, 13, 15) sts. Finish row. Turn work.
   - Dec 1 st at neck edge. Finish row. Turn work.

   - BO 13 (13, 14, 15) sts. Finish row. Turn work.
   - Work across row. Turn work.
   - BO last 13 (14, 14, 15) sts.

8. Complete back neck and shoulder shaping:
   - Join yarn at neck edge and dec 1 st. Finish row. Turn work.
   - BO 13 (13, 14, 15) sts. Finish row. Turn work.
   - Work across row. Turn work.
   - BO last 13 (14, 14, 15) sts.

FRONT

1. Work front exactly the same as back until work measures 13 (15, 17, 19)" from bottom.

2. Beg front neck shaping, remembering to complete armhole shaping at same time:

   Small: Work halfway across the row. Inc 1 st (M1) at exact center front and place this st on a safety pin. Complete right front from this point by dec 1 st at neck edge EOR 26 times.

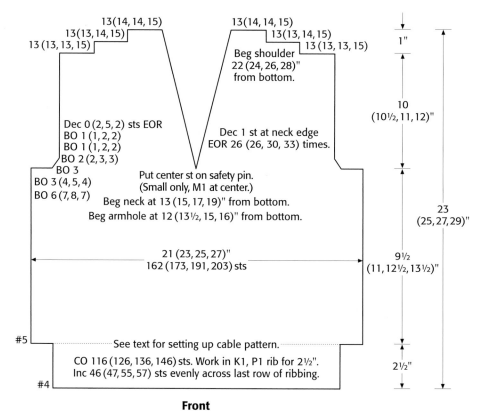

13 (14, 14, 15)
13 (13, 14, 15)
13 (13, 13, 15)

13 (14, 14, 15)
13 (13, 14, 15)
13 (13, 13, 15)

Beg shoulder 22 (24, 26, 28)" from bottom.

1"

10 (10½, 11, 12)"

Dec 0 (2, 5, 2) sts EOR
BO 1 (1, 2, 2)
BO 1 (1, 2, 2)
BO 2 (2, 3, 3)
BO 3
BO 3 (4, 5, 4)
BO 6 (7, 8, 7)

Dec 1 st at neck edge EOR 26 (26, 30, 33) times.

Put center st on safety pin. (Small only, M1 at center.)
Beg neck at 13 (15, 17, 19)" from bottom.
Beg armhole at 12 (13½, 15, 16)" from bottom.

23 (25, 27, 29)"

21 (23, 25, 27)"
162 (173, 191, 203) sts

9½ (11, 12½, 13½)"

#5
See text for setting up cable pattern.
CO 116 (126, 136, 146) sts. Work in K1, P1 rib for 2½". Inc 46 (47, 55, 57) sts evenly across last row of ribbing.
#4

2½"

Front

Medium/Large/X-large: Work halfway across the row. Place the center st on a safety pin. Complete right front from this point by dec 1 st at neck edge EOR 26 (30, 33) times.

3. Cont until work measures 22 (24, 26, 28)" from bottom.

4. Beg shoulder shaping:
   - BO 13 (13, 13, 15) sts at outside edge. Finish row. Turn work.
   - Work across row. Turn work.
   - BO 13 (13, 14, 15) sts. Finish row. Turn work.
   - Work across row. Turn work.
   - BO last 13 (14, 14, 15) sts.

5. Complete left front same as right front, but reverse shaping.

FINISHING

1. Sew shoulder seams. (If the BO took place more than 4 rows after twisting any of the cables, you will probably need to draw in the shoulders slightly as you sew them together to get the desired width.)

2. With RS facing and #4 needles, pick up a total of 156 sts:
   - Pick up 47 sts across back neck from shoulder to shoulder.
   - Pick up 54 sts from right shoulder to point of V; pick up center st, leaving pin in center st.
   - Pick up 54 sts from V to left shoulder.

3. To complete V-neck rib with single st at V, work to last st before center (marked) st and sl that st as if to purl.
   - Put center st on a safety pin (to front of work), knit slipped st and the st to the left of center together as one.
   - Sl this st temporarily to right-hand needle so you can sl center (marked) st back onto right-hand needle.
   - Now PSSO center (marked) st over this st. (Rep this dec every other time you come to the V.)
   - Work in rib pattern for 1½". BO loosely.

4. With RS facing and #4 needles, pick up 122 (128, 134, 144) sts for each armhole. Work in K1, P1 rib for 1". BO loosely. (Chinese BO is optional; see page 137.)

5. Sew side seams.

6. Block sweater to desired measurements.

7. Stabilize back neck and shoulders.

> **TIP**
>
> Use two separate row counters to keep track of alternating cable twists when knitting multiple cables.

TERRY'S RIBBED PULLOVER

We're sure that Terry's favorite sweater is one of a number that his wife, Robin, knit for him, but we hope this is one he'll enjoy for many Sun Valley winters to come. If we were to hire a professional cheerleader for Tricoter, it might very well be Terry. His love for (and success in) retail is a constant inspiration for us. He's one of the few men we know who are more comfortable in our store when there is "standing room only" and the pace is frantic! Having been fortunate (and successful) enough to enjoy the luxury of early retirement, Terry spends a good deal of his time cycling and/or skiing around the world. He will drop in for a retail "fix" between trips, always wanting to know if we're watching the bottom line and reminding us to sell more and buy less. We are continually grateful for the invaluable advice and support that both Robin and Terry have given us over the years, and this sweater is a token of our appreciation and affection. This sweater is already a favorite in our store!

SIZES

Small (Medium, Large, X-Large)
Finished Chest: 42 (46, 50, 54)"
Finished Length: 24 (26, 28, 30)"

MATERIALS

Use a yarn that knits at 4.25 sts to 1".
11 (12, 13, 14) skeins of Noro Kureyon, 100%
   wool, each approximately 110 yds [1210
   (1320, 1430, 1540) yds total]
#6 and #7 needles
Stitch holders

GAUGE

17 sts and 24 rows = 4" in rib pattern on #7
   needles (after steaming)
Always check gauge before starting sweater.
   Increase or decrease needle size to obtain
   correct gauge.

RIB PATTERN

Row 1 (WS): K1, P3, *K1, P5*; rep from * to
   *, end K1, P3, K1 (includes edge sts).
On remaining rows, work sts as they face you,
   remembering to always knit the edge sts.

BACK

1. With #7 needles, CO 93 (99, 105,
    111) sts. Work in rib pattern until
    work measures 13½ (15, 16½, 18)"
    from bottom [21 (23, 25, 27)" wide].

2. At same time that you beg armhole
    shaping, change to a P1, K2 rib. (To
    convert from P1, K5 to P1, K2 rib,
    the center or 3rd knit st in every K5
    now becomes a purl st.)
    ◆ BO 5 sts at beg of next 2 rows.
    ◆ BO 3 sts at beg of next 2 rows.
    ◆ Dec 1 st at beg of next 6 rows
      [71 (77, 83, 89) sts; 16½ (18,
      19½, 21)" wide].

3. Cont in P1, K2 rib until work meas-
    ures 23 (25, 27, 29)" from bottom.

4. Beg back neck and shoulder shaping:
    ◆ BO first 6 (7, 8, 8) sts. Work next
    14 (15, 16, 17) sts. Keeping 15 (16,
    17, 18) sts on right-hand needle, BO

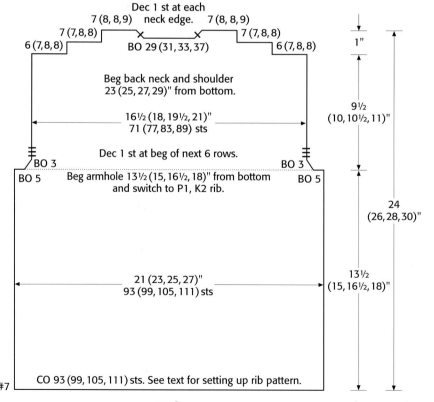

Back

center 29 (31, 33, 37) sts. Finish row. Turn work.

• BO first 6 (7, 8, 8) sts. Finish row. Turn work.

• Dec 1 st at neck edge. Finish row. Turn work.

• BO 7 (7, 8, 8) sts. Finish row. Turn work.

• Work across row. Turn work.

• BO last 7 (8, 8, 9) sts.

5. Complete back neck and shoulder shaping:

• Join yarn at neck edge. Dec 1 st and finish row. Turn work.

• BO 7 (7, 8, 8) sts. Finish row. Turn work.

• Work across row. Turn work.

• BO last 7 (8, 8, 9) sts.

FRONT

1. Work front exactly the same as back until work measures 17 (19, 20, 22)" from bottom.

2. Beg V-neck shaping:

• Place first 35 (38, 41, 44) sts on a stitch holder.

• Place center st on a safety pin and beg dec 1 st at neck edge EOR 15 (16, 17, 19) times.

• Cont in pattern until work measures 23 (25, 27, 29)" from bottom.

3. Beg shoulder shaping:

• BO first 6 (7, 8, 8) sts. Finish row. Turn work.

• Work across row. Turn work.

• BO 7 (7, 8, 8) sts. Finish row. Turn work.

• Work across row. Turn work.

• BO last 7 (8, 8, 9) sts.

4. Work right side the same as left side, but reverse shaping.

SLEEVES

1. With #6 needles, CO 39 (45, 51, 57) sts. Work in rib pattern for 2".

2. Switch to #7 needles and cont in established rib pattern, inc 1 st at each end every 6 (6, 7, 7) rows 18 times [75 (81, 87, 93) sts; 17 (18, 19, 20)" wide].

3. Cont until work measures 17½ (18½, 19½, 20½)" from bottom.

4. Beg cap shaping. At the same time, switch to a P1, K2 rib. (To convert from P1, K5 to P1, K2 rib, the center or 3rd knit st in every K5 now becomes a purl st.)

• BO 5 sts at beg of next 2 rows.

• BO 3 sts at beg of next 4 rows.

• BO 2 sts at beg of next 18 (12, 12, 6) rows.

• BO 3 sts at beg of next 0 (6, 6, 12) rows.

• BO last 17 (17, 23, 23) sts.

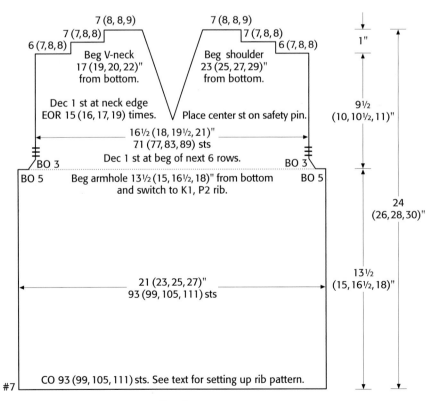

Front

FINISHING

1. Sew shoulder seams.

2. With RS facing and #6 needles, start at center front point of V-neck and pick up a total of 116 (119, 128, 131) sts:
   - Pick up 1 st from safety pin.
   - Pick up 40 (40, 43, 43) sts from point of V to right shoulder.
   - Pick up 35 (38, 41, 44) sts across back neck to left shoulder.
   - Pick up 40 (40, 43, 43) sts from left shoulder to point of V.

3. Because this V-neck crosses rather than meets in the front, turn and work back across row in K1, P1 rib to opposite end of row. (You are working back and forth across the row—*not* in the round.)

4. Cont in K1, P1 rib until work measures 1½". BO.

5. Fold left front over right front of rib at point of V and blindstitch to secure.

6. Sew sleeves in place. Sew side and sleeve seams.

7. Block sweater to desired measurements.

8. Stabilize back neck and shoulders.

TIP

When knitting with space-dyed yarns, such as Kureyon, to get the striping on the sleeves to match, go to the same place in the color sequence on your first skein of yarn when starting the second sleeve as you were on the skein that you used to start your first sleeve. Many people love the random striping that occurs naturally, so this is a tip for those who prefer a little more symmetry.

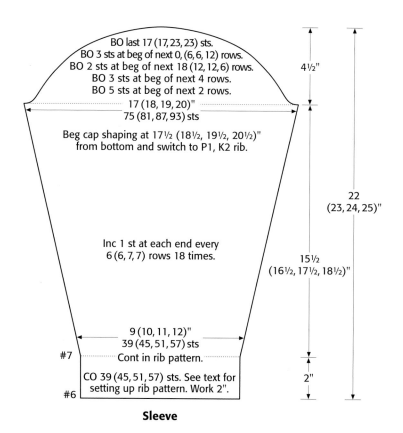

BO last 17 (17, 23, 23) sts.
BO 3 sts at beg of next 0, (6, 6, 12) rows.
BO 2 sts at beg of next 18 (12, 12, 6) rows.
BO 3 sts at beg of next 4 rows.
BO 5 sts at beg of next 2 rows.

4½"

17 (18, 19, 20)"
75 (81, 87, 93) sts

Beg cap shaping at 17½ (18½, 19½, 20½)" from bottom and switch to P1, K2 rib.

22 (23, 24, 25)"

Inc 1 st at each end every 6 (6, 7, 7) rows 18 times.

15½ (16½, 17½, 18½)"

9 (10, 11, 12)"
39 (45, 51, 57) sts

#7   Cont in rib pattern.

CO 39 (45, 51, 57) sts. See text for setting up rib pattern. Work 2".
#6

2"

Sleeve

MEN'S THROW

Men are generally skeptical about the need for a throw, particularly when it is presented as a color-coordinated accessory to complete a new or newly redecorated home. But we have found that men are usually the first ones to use a throw, treating it in much the same manner as an old blanket. We all love the cozy warmth throws provide while reading or watching a game on TV on a chilly afternoon. We have included this throw because it has lots of character and no frills—our favorite throw for men. The tassels add personality without femininity.

ONE SIZE: 44" x 60"

MATERIALS

3 fine yarns that knit together as one, or 1
bulky yarn that knits at 3.55 sts to 1" in
St st.

66 skeins of Baruffa Bollicina, 65% cashmere
and 35% silk, in single color running three
strands together (9750 yds total) or 22
skeins each of taupe #8, brown #9, and
gold #12 (3190 yds total for each); run
three strands together.

#10½ and #10¾ circular turbo needles (47")
Cable needle

GAUGE

28 sts and 22 rows = 4" in pattern stitch on
#10¾ needles

Always check gauge before starting project.
Increase or decrease needle size to obtain
correct gauge.

CABLE PATTERN

(multiple of 24 sts + 2 edge sts)

Row 1 (RS): K1 (edge), *P2, K2*; rep from *
to *, end K1 (edge).

Row 2 (WS): K1, *K2, P2*; rep from * to *,
end K1.

Rows 3–12: Rep rows 1 and 2.

Row 13 (RS): K1, *work 24 sts in established
rib pattern. Put next 12 sts on cable needle
and hold to back of work. Work next 12 sts
in rib, work 12 sts off cable needle*; rep
from * to * 5 more times, work 24 sts in
established rib pattern, K1. From this point,
twist each of these cables every 24 rows.

Rows 14–24: Cont rib pattern.

Row 25: K1, *place next 12 sts on cable needle and hold to back of work. Work next
12 sts in rib, work 12 sts off cable needle.
Work next 24 sts in established rib pattern*; rep from * to * 5 more times. Place
next 12 sts on cable needle and hold to
back of work. Work next 12 sts in rib, work

12 sts off cable needle, K1. From this point,
twist each of these cables every 24 rows.

DIRECTIONS

1. With #10½ needles, CO 314 sts.
   Switch to #10¾ needles and follow
   cable pattern (13 cables).

2. When work measures 60" from bottom, switch to #10½ needles and BO
   firmly.

FINISHING

Block throw to desired dimensions.

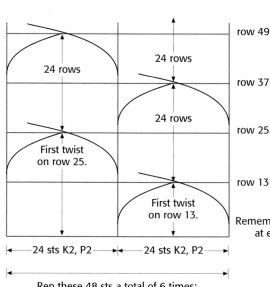

row 49

24 rows

24 rows

row 37

24 rows

24 rows

row 25

First twist
on row 25.

row 13

First twist
on row 13.

Remember 1 edge st
at each side.

|← 24 sts K2, P2 →|← 24 sts K2, P2 →|

Rep these 48 sts a total of 6 times;
then rep the first 24 sts one more time.

ALAN'S PASHMINA MUFFLER

This muffler is dedicated to Alan and the best "how to meet a woman" strategy we've yet encountered. A mutual friend had mentioned Beryl to his good friend Alan, knowing that she was, at that time, single. Alan stopped in to Tricoter on a very hot summer day, braving the tables of women knitting to meet the woman he was certain could design the perfect cashmere muffler to match his winter coat. The romance didn't last, but our appreciation for the creativity to make a private appointment for a consultation on a custom-knit muffler hasn't faded with time.

ONE SIZE: 7" x 60"

MATERIALS

A fine yarn that knits at 6.0 sts to 1" in St st.

3 skeins of Great Adirondack hand-dyed
Pashmina, each approximately 250 yds [750
yds total]

#6 and #8 needles

Cable needle

GAUGE

46 sts and 36 rows = 4" in pattern stitch on
#8 needles

Always check gauge before starting project.
Increase or decrease needle size to obtain
correct gauge.

CABLE PATTERN

(multiple of 24 plus 8 for 4-st garter border
on each side)

Row 1 (RS): K4. *P2, K2*; rep from * to *,
end K4.

Row 2 (WS): K4, *P2, K2*; rep from * to *,
end K4.

Rows 3–12: Rep rows 1 and 2.

Row 13 (RS): K4, work next 24 sts in established rib pattern. Put next 12 sts on cable
needle and hold to back of work. Work
next 12 sts in rib pattern. Work 12 sts off
cable needle. Work next 24 sts in established rib pattern, K4. From this point, twist
center cable every 24 rows.

Rows 14–24: Cont in rib pattern.

Row 25: K4, place next 12 sts on cable needle
and hold to back of work. Work next 12 sts
in rib pattern, work 12 sts off cable needle.
Work next 24 sts in established rib pattern,
place next 12 sts on cable needle and hold
to back of work, work next 12 sts in rib
pattern, work 12 sts off cable needle, K4.
From this point, twist outside cables every
24 rows.

DIRECTIONS

1. With #6 needle, CO 80 sts. Switch to
   #8 needles and follow cable pattern.

2. When work measures 60" from bottom, switch to #6 needles and BO
   firmly.

FINISHING

Block muffler to desired dimensions.

> ### TIP
>
> For a more feminine version
> of this muffler, draw the fin-
> ished ends of the muffler
> together and attach a tassel
> to each end (see "Tips for
> Technicians" on page 137).

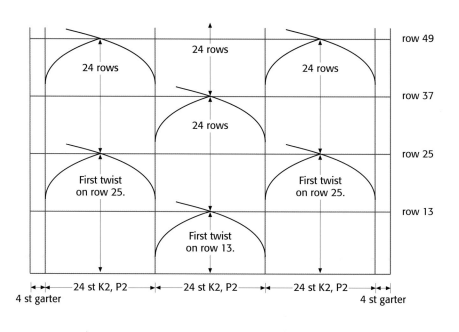

THE BUSINESS AT HAND

"We are confronted with insurmountable opportunities." —POGO

The casual-dress culture epitomized by Microsoft in the last decade seems to have invaded even the most historically conservative businesses in the new millennium. While suits may have been replaced by sweaters and slacks in the office, the concepts of luxury and quiet quality have become even more important as a mark of professional status. The style is generally classic, but the subtle detailing has a very contemporary edge. Comfort is a prime consideration, and the growing number of luxury fibers available for hand knitting makes the process of knitting as enjoyable as the completed sweater.

PATRICK'S SILK RIBBED PULLOVER

Patrick has been our personal trainer, advisor, confidant, design consultant, party planner extraordinaire, unofficial PR man, and true friend for a number of years. In recognition of his superb capability in balancing all of those hats and maintaining a calm and generous spirit through it all, we have designed this sleek, sophisticated sweater that reflects the simplicity and clean lines defining Patrick's environment. This is a sweater you'll love to knit in a luxury fiber!

SIZES

Small (Medium, Large, X-Large)
Finished Chest: 42 (46, 50, 54)"
Finished Length: 24 (26, 28, 30)"

MATERIALS

Use a yarn that knits at 4.75 sts to 1" in St st.
14 (15, 16, 22) skeins of Lang Cocoon, 80%
  silk and 20% nylon, each approximately
  105 yds [1470 (1575, 1680, 1785) yds total]
#4 and #6 needles

GAUGE

21 sts and 26½ rows = 4" in rib pattern on
  #6 needles
Always check gauge before starting sweater.
  Increase or decrease needle size to obtain
  correct gauge.

RIB PATTERN

Row 1: *K4, P2*; rep from * to *.
Row 2: Work sts as they face you across the
  row.

BACK

1. With #4 needles, CO 110 (122, 134,
   146) sts. Set up rib pattern (includes
   edge sts):

   Row 1 (WS): K1 (edge st), P2, *K2,
   P4*; rep from * to *, end K2, P2, K1
   (edge st).

   Row 2 (RS): K3, *P2, K4*; rep from *
   to *, end P2, K3.

   Work in pattern for 2".

2. Switch to #6 needles and cont in rib
   pattern until work measures 13½ (15,
   16½, 18)" from bottom [21 (23, 25,
   27)" wide].

3. Beg armhole shaping:
   ◆ BO 3 (3, 5, 5) sts at beg of next 2
   rows.
   ◆ BO 2 (2, 4, 4) sts at beg of next 2
   rows.
   ◆ BO 2 sts at beg of next 2 rows.
   ◆ Dec 1 st at beg of next 6 rows
   [90 (102, 106, 118) sts; 17 (19, 22½,
   25)" wide].

4. Cont until work measures 23 (25, 27,
   29)" from bottom.

5. Beg back neck and shoulder shaping:
   ◆ BO first 9 (10, 10, 12) sts. Work
   next 18 (21, 22, 24) sts. Keeping 19
   (22, 23, 25) sts on right-hand nee-
   dle, BO center 34 (38, 40, 44) sts.
   Finish row. Turn work.
   ◆ BO first 9 (10, 10, 12) sts. Finish
   row. Turn work.
   ◆ Dec 1 st at neck edge. Finish row.
   Turn work.
   ◆ BO 9 (10, 11, 12) sts. Finish row.
   Turn work.

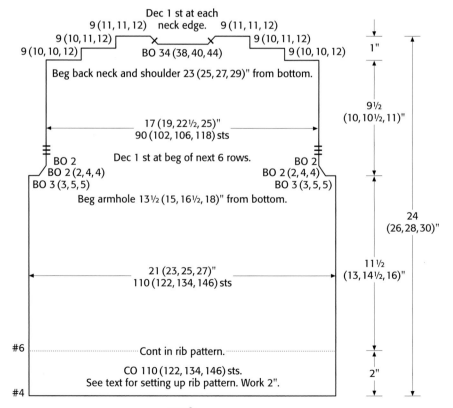

Dec 1 st at each neck edge.
9 (11, 11, 12)   9 (11, 11, 12)
9 (10, 11, 12)   9 (10, 11, 12)
9 (10, 10, 12)   BO 34 (38, 40, 44)   9 (10, 10, 12)
1"

Beg back neck and shoulder 23 (25, 27, 29)" from bottom.

17 (19, 22½, 25)"
90 (102, 106, 118) sts
9½ (10, 10½, 11)"

BO 2   Dec 1 st at beg of next 6 rows.   BO 2
BO 2 (2, 4, 4)   BO 2 (2, 4, 4)
BO 3 (3, 5, 5)   BO 3 (3, 5, 5)

Beg armhole 13½ (15, 16½, 18)" from bottom.

24 (26, 28, 30)"

21 (23, 25, 27)"
110 (122, 134, 146) sts
11½ (13, 14½, 16)"

#6   Cont in rib pattern.

CO 110 (122, 134, 146) sts.
See text for setting up rib pattern. Work 2".
2"
#4

Back

- ◆ Work across row. Turn work.
- ◆ BO last 9 (11, 11, 12) sts.

6. Complete back neck and shoulder shaping:
   - ◆ Join yarn at neck edge. Dec 1 st and finish row. Turn work.
   - ◆ BO 9 (10, 11, 12) sts. Finish row. Turn work.
   - ◆ Work across row. Turn work.
   - ◆ BO last 9 (11, 11, 12) sts.

FRONT

1. Work front exactly the same as back until work measures 21 (23, 25, 27)" from bottom.

2. Beg front neck shaping:
   - ◆ Work first 33 (39, 41, 47) sts. BO center 24 (28, 30, 34) sts. Finish row. Turn work.
   - ◆ Work across row. Turn work.
   - ◆ Dec 1 st at neck edge EOR 6 times.

3. Cont until work measures 23 (25, 27, 29)" from bottom.

4. Beg shoulder shaping:
   - ◆ BO 9 (10, 10, 12) sts at outside edge. Finish row. Turn work.
   - ◆ Work across row. Turn work.
   - ◆ BO 9 (10, 11, 12) sts. Finish row. Turn work.

- ◆ Work across row. Turn work.
- ◆ BO last 9 (11, 11, 12) sts.

5. Complete front neck shaping:
   - ◆ Join yarn at neck edge. Dec 1 st and finish row. Turn work.
   - ◆ Work across row. Turn work.
   - ◆ Dec 1 st at neck edge EOR 5 times.

6. Complete shoulder shaping as in step 4.

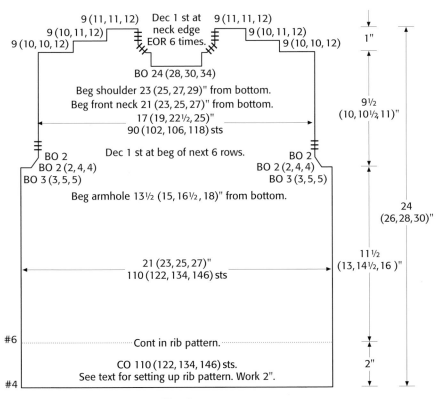

Front

SLEEVES

1. With #4 needles, CO 46 (48, 52, 54) sts. Set up rib pattern (includes edge sts). Row 1 (WS):

   Small/Large: K2, *P4, K2*; rep from * to *, end P1, K1.

   Medium/X-Large: K3, *P4, K2*; rep from * to *, end P2, K1.

   Work in pattern for 2".

2. Switch to #6 needles and cont in established rib pattern, inc 1 st at each end every 4 rows 25 (26, 27, 28) times, remembering to maintain rib pattern [96 (100, 106, 110) sts; 18 (19, 20, 21)" wide].

3. Cont until work measures 18 (19, 20, 21)" from bottom.

4. Beg cap shaping:
   - BO 3 (3, 5, 5) sts at beg of next 2 rows.
   - BO 2 (2, 4, 4) sts at beg of next 2 rows.
   - BO 2 sts at beg of next 2 rows.
   - BO 3 sts at beg of next 8 rows.
   - BO 4 (4, 3, 4) sts at beg of next 4 rows.
   - BO 4 sts at beg of next 6 rows.
   - BO last 18 (22, 24, 24) sts.

FINISHING

1. Sew shoulder seams, matching ribs on front and back.

2. With RS facing and #4 needles, pick up a total of 96 (96, 108, 108) sts:
   - Pick up 40 (40, 46, 46) sts across back neck from shoulder to shoulder.
   - Pick up 56 (56, 62, 62) sts across front neck from shoulder to shoulder.

3. Set up K4, P2 rib pattern, being careful to match knit and purl sts on neck to those on body of sweater. Work in rib pattern for 2". BO loosely.

4. Sew in sleeves. Sew side and sleeve seams.

5. Block sweater to desired measurements.

6. Stabilize back neck and shoulders.

BO last 18 (22, 24, 24) sts.
BO 4 sts at beg of next 6 rows.
BO 4 (4, 3, 4) sts at beg of next 4 rows.
BO 3 sts at beg of next 8 rows.
BO 2 sts at beg of next 2 rows.
BO 2 (2, 4, 4) sts at beg of next 2 rows.
BO 3 (3, 5, 5) sts at beg of next 2 rows.

18 (19, 20, 21)"
96 (100, 106, 110) sts

Beg cap shaping at 18 (19, 20, 21)" from bottom.

Inc 1 st at each end every 4 rows 25 (26, 27, 28) times.

4"

22 (23, 24, 25)"

16 (17, 18, 19)"

8½ (9, 9½, 10)"
46 (48, 52, 54) sts

#6 · · · · Cont in rib pattern.

CO 46 (48, 52, 54) sts. See text for setting up pattern. Work 2".

#4

2"

Sleeve

TIP

As you work across the row, it is important to keep the 4th knit stitch as firm as possible. It is a normal tendency to work this stitch a little looser; keeping it firm will give your work a more consistent look.

STACY'S SWEATER

Designing a sweater for the man who supplies us with the most luxurious and beautiful fibers from around the world and whose personal style is impeccable is an intimidating challenge. We loved these thick, ropy cables and classic styling with a subtle twist.

Somehow, Zara, one of the beautiful classic "luxury basics" staples in Stacy's Filatura di Crosa line for a number of years, seemed the perfect yarn. This sweater would also be beautiful in cashmere. Stacy, we hope that you enjoy this sweater as much as we have enjoyed making it for you!

SIZES

Small (Medium, Large, X-Large)
Finished Chest: 43 (46, 51, 56)"
Finished Length: 21 (23, 25, 27)"

MATERIALS

Use a yarn that knits at 4.75 sts to 1" in St st.
13 (14, 15, 16) skeins of Filatura di Crosa
    Zara, 100% merino extra fine wool, each
    approximately 136 yds [1768 (1904, 2040,
    2176) yds total], in the following colors:
        12 (13, 14, 15) skeins of charcoal #1469
        1 skein of taupe #1477
#4 and #6 needles
Cable needle

GAUGE

40 sts and 26 rows = 4" in cable/stockinette
    pattern on #6 needles
Always check gauge before starting sweater.
    Increase or decrease needle size to obtain
    correct gauge.

CABLE PATTERN

Note: The first 5 rows are to set up the cable
    coming out of *K3, P1* rib.
Row 1 (RS): P1, K3, P1, K3, P1 [9 sts].
Row 2 (WS): K1, P3, K1, P3, K1.
Row 3: P1, K3, M1, K3, P1.
Row 4: K1, *P1, M1*; rep from * to * 7
    times, end K1 [18 sts].
Row 5: P1, C8F, P1.
Rows 6, 8, 10, 12, 14: K1, P16, K1.
Rows 7, 9, 11, 13: P1, K16, P1.
Row 15: Rep row 5.
Rep rows 6–15.

BACK

1. With #4 needles and charcoal, CO 89
   (97, 109, 121) sts. Set up rib pattern:
   - Row 1 (WS): K1, P3, K1, *P3,
   K1*; rep from * to *, end P3, K1.
   - Work 3 rows in K3, P1 rib.

2. On 4th (RS) row, add taupe and work
   next 2 rows in color-work pattern:

   K3 in taupe, P1 in charcoal; rep
   from * to * across row. (On 5th row,
   work sts as they face you in color-
   work pattern.)

3. Return to charcoal and cont in rib
   pattern until work measures 2" from
   bottom. End on WS row.

4. Switch to #6 needles and set up body
   of sweater (setup row includes edge
   sts):

   Row 1 for Small: K4, *P1, K3, P1,
   K3, P1, K15*; rep from * to * 2 more
   times, end P1, K3, P1, K3, P1, K4
   [89 sts].

   Row 1 for Medium: K4, P1, K3, P1,
   K3, P1, K19, P1, K3, P1, K3, P1,
   K15, P1, K3, P1, K3, P1, K19, P1,
   K3, P1, K3, P1, K4 [97 sts].

   Row 1 for Large: K8, *P1, K3, P1,
   K3, P1, K19*; rep from * to * 2 more
   times, end P1, K3, P1, K3, P1, K8
   [109 sts].

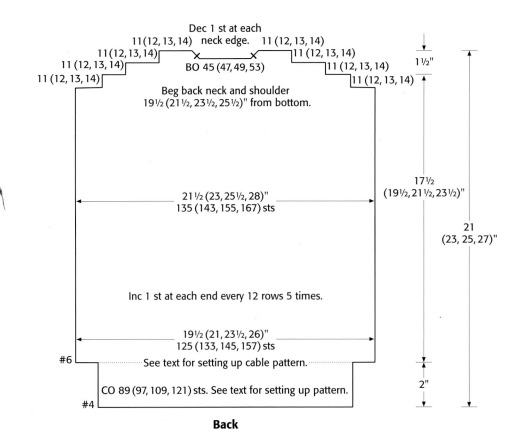

Back

Row 1 for X-Large: K8, *P1, K3, P1, K3, P1, K23*; rep from * to * 2 more times, end P1, K3, P1, K3, P1, K8 [121 sts].

Row 2: Work all sts as they face you.

Row 3: Each of the 4 times you come to the P1, K3, P1, K3, P1 sequence in this row, M1 after the 2nd of the 3 purl sts as follows: P1, K3, P1, M1, K3, P1 [93 (101, 113, 125) sts].

Row 4 (WS): Each of the 4 times you come to the K1, P3, K1, P4, K1 sequence in this row, work it as follows: K1, *P1, M1*; rep from * to * 7 times, K1 (you are increasing 8 sts into each cable on this row) [125 (133, 145, 157) sts].

Row 5 for Small: K4, *P1, C8F, P1, K15*; rep from * to * 2 more times, end P1, C8F, P1, K4.

Row 5 for Medium: K4, P1, C8F, P1, K19, P1, C8F, P1, K15, P1, C8F, P1, K19, P1, C8F, P1, K4.

Row 5 for Large: K8, *P1, C8F, P1, K19*; rep from * to * 2 more times, end P1, C8F, P1, K8.

Row 5 for X-Large: K8, *P1, C8F, P1, K23*; rep from * to * 2 more times, end P1, C8F, P1, K8.

Cont working sts as they face you, remembering to twist the 4 cables on every 10th (RS) row.

5. Inc 1 st at each end every 12 rows 5 times [135 (143, 155, 167) sts; 21½ (23, 25½, 28)" wide].

6. Cont until work measures 19½ (21½, 23½, 25½)" from bottom.

7. Beg back neck and shoulder shaping:
    ◆ BO first 11 (12, 13, 14) sts. Finish row. Turn work.
    ◆ BO first 11 (12, 13, 14) sts. Finish row. Turn work.
    ◆ BO 11 (12, 13, 14) sts. Work next 22 (24, 26, 28) sts. Keeping 23 (25, 27, 29) sts on right-hand needle, BO center 45 (47, 49, 53) sts. Finish row. Turn work.
    ◆ BO 11 (12, 13, 14) sts. Finish row to neck edge. Turn work.
    ◆ Dec 1 st at neck edge. Finish row. Turn work.
    ◆ BO 11 (12, 13, 14) sts. Finish row. Turn work.
    ◆ Work across row. Turn work.
    ◆ BO last 11 (12, 13, 14) sts.

8. Complete back neck and shoulder shaping:
    ◆ Join yarn at neck edge and dec 1 st. Finish row. Turn work.
    ◆ BO 11 (12, 13, 14) sts. Finish row. Turn work.
    ◆ Work across row. Turn work.
    ◆ BO last 11 (12, 13, 14) sts.

FRONT

1. Work front exactly the same as back until work measures 18½ (20½, 21½, 23½)" from bottom.

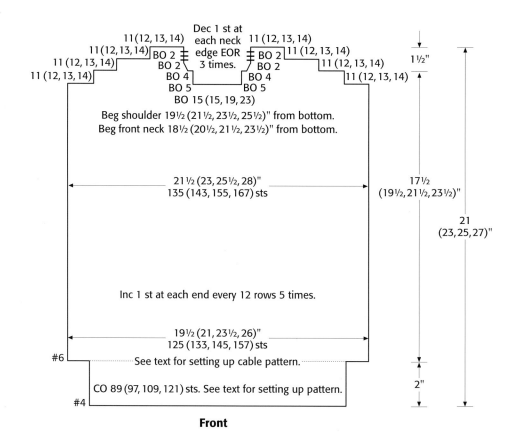

Front

2. Beg front neck shaping:
   ◆ Work first 60 (64, 68, 72) sts. BO center 15 (15, 19, 23) sts. Finish row. Turn work.
   ◆ Work across row. Turn work.
   ◆ BO 5 sts at neck edge. Finish row. Turn work.
   ◆ Work across row. Turn work.
   ◆ BO 4 sts at neck edge. Finish row. Turn work.
   ◆ BO 2 sts at neck edge EOR 2 times.
   ◆ Dec 1 st at neck edge EOR 3 times.

3. Cont until work measures 19½ (21½, 23½, 25½)" from bottom.

4. Beg shoulder shaping:
   ◆ BO first 11 (12, 13, 14) sts at outside edge. Finish row. Turn work.
   ◆ Work across row. Turn work.
   ◆ BO 11 (12, 13, 14) sts. Finish row. Turn work.
   ◆ Work across row. Turn work.
   ◆ BO 11 (12, 13, 14) sts. Finish row. Turn work.
   ◆ Work across row. Turn work.
   ◆ BO last 11 (12, 13, 14) sts.

5. Complete front neck shaping:
   ◆ Join yarn at neck edge. BO first 5 sts. Finish row. Turn work.
   ◆ Work across row. Turn work.
   ◆ BO 4 sts at neck edge. Finish row. Turn work.
   ◆ BO 2 sts at neck edge EOR 2 times.
   ◆ Dec 1 st at neck edge EOR 3 times.

Cont until work measures 19½ (21½, 23½, 25½)" from bottom.

6. Complete shoulder shaping as in step 4 above.

SLEEVES

1. With #4 needles and charcoal, CO 47 (47, 55, 55) sts:

   Row 1 (WS): K2, P3, *K1, P3*; rep from * to *, end K2. (Setup row includes edge sts.)

   Row 2: Work sts as they face you.

   Work 1 more row in K3, P1 rib.

2. On 4th (RS) row, add taupe and work next 2 rows in color-work pattern:

   K3 in taupe, P1 in charcoal; rep from * to * across row. (On 5th row, work sts as they face you in color-work pattern.)

3. Return to charcoal and cont in rib pattern until work measures 2" from bottom. Inc 1 st at each end in last row of rib. End on WS row [49 (49, 57, 57) sts].

4. Switch to #6 needles and set up sleeve (setup row includes edge sts):

   Row 1: K18 (18, 22, 22), *P1, K3*; rep from * to * 2 more times, end P1, K18 (18, 22, 22).

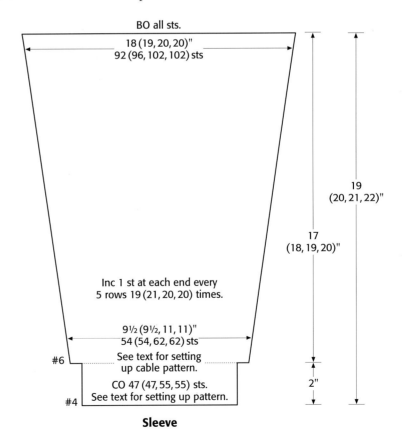

BO all sts.

18 (19, 20, 20)"
92 (96, 102, 102) sts

19 (20, 21, 22)"

17 (18, 19, 20)"

Inc 1 st at each end every 5 rows 19 (21, 20, 20) times.

9½ (9½, 11, 11)"
54 (54, 62, 62) sts

#6

See text for setting up cable pattern.

CO 47 (47, 55, 55) sts.
See text for setting up pattern.

#4

2"

Sleeve

Row 2: Work sts as they face you.

Row 3: K18 (18, 22, 22), P1, K11, P1, K18 (18, 22, 22).

Row 4: K1, P17 (17, 21, 21), K1, P3, *M1, P1*; rep from * to * 4 more times, end P3, K1, P17 (17, 21, 21), K1 (you have now increased 5 sts into the cable) [54 (54, 62, 62) sts].

Row 5: K18 (18, 22, 22), P1, C8F, P1, K18 (18, 22, 22).

Cont working sts as they face you, remembering to twist cable every 10th (RS) row.

5. Inc 1 st at each end every 5th row 19 (21, 20, 20) times [92 (96, 102, 102) sts; 18 (19, 20, 20)" wide].

6. Cont until work measures 19 (20, 21, 22)" from bottom. BO all sts.

FINISHING

1. Sew shoulder seams. (If the BO took place more than 4 rows after twisting any of the cables, you will probably need to draw in the shoulders slightly as you sew them together to get the desired width.)

2. With RS facing, charcoal yarn, and #4 needles, pick up a total of 96 (96, 104, 104) sts:
   - Pick up 44 (44, 48, 48) sts across back neck from shoulder to shoulder.
   - Pick up 52 (52, 56, 56) sts across front neck from shoulder to shoulder.

3. Work in K3, P1 rib for 2½". BO.

4. Fold rib to inside of neck and slip-stitch in place.

5. Sew in sleeves. Sew side and sleeve seams.

6. Block sweater to desired measurements.

7. Stabilize back neck and shoulders.

TIP

When twisting the cables, because of the number of stitches being held, knitting them off the cable needle may be difficult. To make this easier, try using a 16"-long #4 circular needle in place of a traditional cable needle.

DAD'S VEST

I wanted to knit something really special for my father on his seventy-fifth birthday. He's a very distinguished-looking man with silver/white hair and a perennial California tan. Because he enjoys the mild Southern California weather year-round, a vest seemed more appropriate than a sweater. His vest was originally knit in cashmere (it seemed the perfect choice for such an auspicious occasion), but we've translated it here in a wonderful 100% wool from Mission Falls. The "roll" detail at the neck and armholes gives an updated look to a classic vest.—Lindy

SIZES

Small (Medium, Large, X-Large)
Finished Chest: 42 (46, 50, 54)"
Finished Length: 25 (26, 27, 28)"

MATERIALS

Use a yarn that knits at 4.5 sts to 1".
10 (11, 12, 13) total skeins of Mission Hills
   1824 Wool, 100% merino superwash, each
   approximately 85 yds [850 (935, 1020,
   1105) yds total], in the following colors:
      7 (8, 9, 10) skeins of black #05
      1 skein each of red #05, charcoal #15,
      and pearl gray #07
Stitch holders

GAUGE

18 sts and 24 rows = 4" in St st on #7 needles
Always check gauge before starting sweater.
   Increase or decrease needle size to obtain
   correct gauge.

BACK

1. With #5 needles and black yarn, CO
   88 (96, 106, 114) sts. Work 1 row in
   K1, P1 rib.
   ♦ Switch to red and work 1 row in
   rib.
   ♦ Switch to black and cont in rib
   until work measures 2½" from bottom. End with a WS row.

2. Switch to #7 needles and work 1 row
   in St st with black.

3. Work 4-row color-work pattern:
   ♦ Work 1 row with red.

   ♦ Work next 2 rows in 1 st charcoal,
   2 sts pearl gray color-work pattern.
   ♦ Work 1 row with red.

4. Switch to black and cont in St st, inc
   1 st at each end every 2" 4 (5, 4, 5)
   times [96 (106, 114, 124) sts; 21 (23,
   25, 27)" wide].

5. Cont until work measures 14½ (15,
   15, 15)" from bottom.

6. Beg armhole shaping:
   ♦ BO 5 (5, 7, 7) sts at beg of next 2
   rows.
   ♦ BO 3 (4, 4, 5) sts at beg of next 2
   rows.

   ♦ Dec 1 st at beg of next 6 (10, 10,
   12) rows [74 (78, 82, 88) sts; 16 (17,
   18, 19)" wide].

7. Cont until work measures 24 (25, 26,
   27)" from bottom.

8. Beg back neck and shoulder shaping:
   ♦ BO first 7 sts. Work across next 14
   (14, 15, 16) sts. Keeping 15 (15, 16,
   17) sts on right-hand needle, BO
   center 30 (34, 38, 42) sts. Finish
   row. Turn work.
   ♦ BO first 7 sts. Finish row to neck
   edge. Turn work.

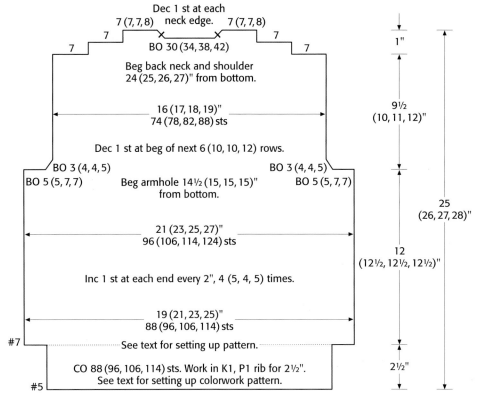

Back

◆ Dec 1 st at neck edge. Finish row. Turn work.

◆ BO 7 sts. Finish row. Turn work.

◆ Work across row. Turn work.

◆ BO last 7 (7, 7, 8) sts.

9. Complete back neck and shoulder shaping:

◆ Join yarn at neck edge. Dec 1 st and finish row. Turn work.

◆ BO 7 sts. Finish row. Turn work.

◆ Work across row. Turn work.

◆ BO last 7 (7, 7, 8) sts.

FRONT

1. Work front exactly the same as back until work measures 17 (18, 19, 20)" from bottom [74 (78, 82, 88) sts; 16 (17, 18, 19)" wide].

2. Beg V-neck shaping:

◆ Place first 36 (38, 40, 43) sts on a stitch holder.

◆ Place center 2 sts on a safety pin and finish the row. Turn work.

◆ Dec 1 st at neck edge as follows:

Small/Medium: every 3 rows 15 (17) times

Large/X-Large: EOR 19 (21) times.

3. Cont until work measures 24 (25, 26, 27)" from bottom.

4. Beg shoulder shaping:

◆ BO first 7 sts at outside edge. Finish row. Turn work.

◆ Work across row. Turn work.

◆ BO 7 sts. Finish row. Turn work.

◆ Work across row. Turn work.

◆ BO last 7 (7, 7, 8) sts.

5. Join yarn at neck edge and complete left side the same as right side, but reverse shaping.

FINISHING

1. Sew shoulder seams.

2. With RS facing, #5 needles, and red yarn, pick up a total of 107 (109, 119, 121) sts:

◆ Pick up 29 (31, 33, 35) sts across back neck from shoulder to shoulder.

◆ Pick up 38 (38, 42, 42) sts from left shoulder to center.

◆ Pick up 2 center sts, leaving safety pin in sts.

◆ Pick up 38 (38, 42, 42) sts from center back to right shoulder.

◆ Knit 4 more rows with red in St st. BO loosely on 5th row.

3. With RS facing, #5 needles, and black yarn, pick up the same sts from inside edge of red roll. On pickup row, pick up 2 center sts from safety pin as one in pattern [106 (108, 118, 120) sts total].

◆ To complete V-neck in K1, P1 rib with single st at V, work to last st before center (marked) st and sl that st as if to purl.

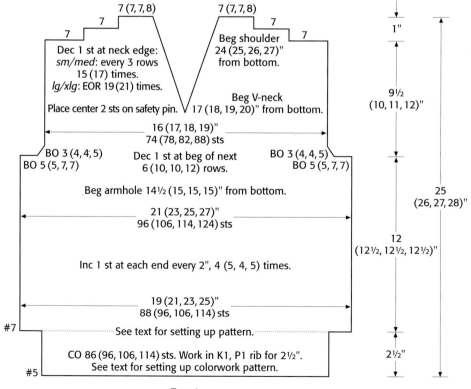

Front

• Put center st on a safety pin (to front of work), knit slipped st and st to left of center together as one.

• Sl this st temporarily to right-hand needle so that you can sl center (marked) st back onto right-hand needle.

• Now PSSO center (marked) st over this st. (Rep this dec every other time you come to the V.)

• Work 3 more rows in black rib pattern.

• Switch to red and work 1 row in rib pattern.

• Switch to black for 1 more row. BO on next row.

4. Complete armhole shaping:

• With RS facing, #5 needles, and red yarn, pick up 100 (104, 112, 120) sts and work 4 more rows in St st. BO loosely on next row.

• With RS facing, #5 needles, and black yarn, pick up again in same sts on inside of red roll. Work 4 rows in K1, P1 rib.

• Switch to red for 1 row.

• Switch to black for 1 more row. BO on next row.

5. Sew side seams.

6. Block vest to desired measurements.

7. Stabilize back neck and shoulders.

TIP

The key to getting the red stockinette stitches at the neck and armholes to roll consistently is to BO loosely. You may want to tack the roll at the side seams to keep it from "relaxing."

HEINZ'S CASHMERE VEST

Ingrid has been a part of Tricoter from the very early days. Her incredible pattern-making skills are the result of a lifetime of knitting, from her childhood in Germany's Black Forest region to her current life here in Seattle. She has made a number of vests for her husband over the years, and when we were discussing the design for a classic men's traditional cardigan vest, Ingrid offered to help with the design. This beautiful, timeless vest is so truly like Heinz that we couldn't resist dedicating it to the man who inspired it. This is another style that women love to wear.

114

SIZES

Small (Medium, Large, X-Large)

Finished Chest: 40 (42, 48, 52)"

Finished Length: 20 (22, 24, 26)"

MATERIALS

Use a yarn that knits at 5 sts to 1".

6 (7, 8, 8) total skeins of Filatura di Crosa,
100% cashmere, each approximately 153
yds [918 (1071, 1224, 1224) yds total], in
the following colors:

    5 (6, 7, 7) skeins of charcoal, color #75

    1 skein of black, color #002

#4 and #6 needles

#4 circular needle (47")

5 (5, 6, 6) buttons, approximately ½" in
diameter

Stitch holders

GAUGE

20 sts and 26 rows = 4" in St st on #6
  needles

Always check gauge before starting sweater.
Increase or decrease needle size to obtain
correct gauge.

BACK

1. With #4 needles, CO 102 (112, 122,
132) sts with black. Work in K1, P1
rib for 1 more row, then switch to
charcoal and cont in rib pattern until
work measures 1½" from bottom.

2. Switch to #6 needles and work in St
st until work measures 10 (11½, 12½,
13½)" from bottom [20 (22, 24, 26)"
wide].

3. Beg armhole shaping:
   - BO 6 (6, 6, 8) sts at beg of next 2
   rows.
   - BO 4 sts at beg of next 2 rows.
   - BO 2 sts at beg of next 4 rows.
   - Dec 1 st at beg of next 2 (8, 12,
   14) rows [72 (76, 82, 86) sts; 14 (15,
   16, 17)" wide].

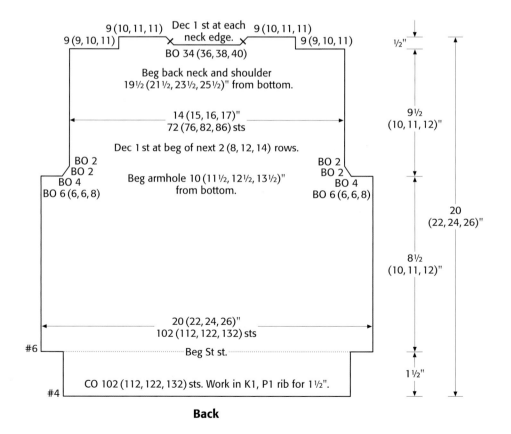

9 (10, 11, 11) Dec 1 st at each 9 (10, 11, 11)

9 (9, 10, 11) neck edge. 9 (9, 10, 11)

BO 34 (36, 38, 40)

Beg back neck and shoulder
19½ (21½, 23½, 25½)" from bottom.

14 (15, 16, 17)"
72 (76, 82, 86) sts

Dec 1 st at beg of next 2 (8, 12, 14) rows.

BO 2   BO 2
BO 2   BO 2
BO 4   BO 4
BO 6 (6, 6, 8)   BO 6 (6, 6, 8)

Beg armhole 10 (11½, 12½, 13½)"
from bottom.

20 (22, 24, 26)"
102 (112, 122, 132) sts

#6   Beg St st.

#4   CO 102 (112, 122, 132) sts. Work in K1, P1 rib for 1½".

½"

9½
(10, 11, 12)"

20
(22, 24, 26)"

8½
(10, 11, 12)"

1½"

Back

4. Cont until work measures 19½ (21½, 23½, 25½)" from bottom.

5. Beg back neck and shoulder shaping:
   ◆ BO first 9 (9, 10, 11) sts. Knit next 10 (11, 12, 12) sts. Keeping 11 (12, 13, 13) sts on right-hand needle, BO center 34 (36, 38, 40) sts. Finish row. Turn work.
   ◆ BO 9 (9, 10, 11) sts. Finish row. Turn work.
   ◆ Dec 1 st at neck edge. Finish row. Turn work.
   ◆ BO last 9 (10, 11, 11) sts.

6. Complete back neck and shoulder shaping:
   ◆ Join yarn at neck edge. Dec 1 st and finish row. Turn work.
   ◆ BO last 9 (10, 11, 11) sts.

FRONTS

1. Knit 2 pocket linings:
   ◆ With #6 needles, CO 23 (23, 27, 27) sts with charcoal.
   ◆ Work in St st for 3½ (3½, 4, 4)". Place on stitch holders and set aside.

2. Beg with right front: With #4 needles and black, CO 50 (54, 60, 66) sts.

Work in K1, P1 rib with black for 1 more row.
   ◆ Switch to charcoal and cont in rib pattern until work measures 1½" from bottom.

3. Switch to #6 needles and work in St st until work measures 5 (5, 5½, 5½)" from bottom.

4. Work pockets. Starting at center front:
   ◆ Knit first 13 (15, 16, 19) sts. Place next 23 (23, 27, 27) sts on a stitch holder.
   ◆ Knit 23 (23, 27, 27) sts of first pocket lining off stitch holder.
   ◆ Knit last 14 (16, 17, 20) sts.

5. Cont until work measures 10 (11½, 12½, 13½)" from bottom [50 (54, 60, 66) sts; 10 (11, 12, 13)" wide].

6. Beg armhole shaping and V-neck shaping at same time (see step 7):
   ◆ BO 6 (6, 6, 8) sts at beg of outside edge. Finish row. Turn work.
   ◆ Work across row. Turn work.
   ◆ BO 4 sts at outside edge. Finish row. Turn work.
   ◆ Work across row. Turn work.
   ◆ BO 2 sts at outside edge EOR 2 times.
   ◆ Dec 1 st at outside edge EOR 1 (4, 6, 7) time.

7. At same time, beg V-neck dec:
   ◆ Dec 1 st at neck edge every 3 (4, 4, 3) rows 17 (17, 19, 21) times.

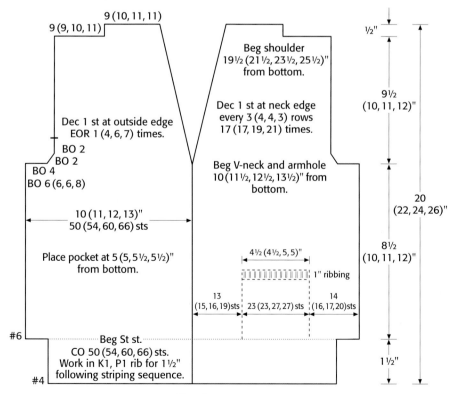

Front

8. Cont until work measures 19½ (21½, 23½, 25½)" from bottom.

9. Beg shoulder shaping:
    - BO 9 (10, 11, 11) sts. Finish row. Turn work.
    - Work across row. Turn work.
    - BO last 9 (10, 11, 11) sts.

10. Work left front the same as right front but reverse shaping.

11. Work left front pocket, starting at side seam:
    - Knit first 14 (16, 17, 20) sts. Place next 23 (23, 27, 27) sts on a stitch holder.
    - Knit 23 (23, 27, 27) sts of first pocket lining off stitch holder.
    - Knit last 13 (15, 16, 19) sts.

FINISHING

1. Sew shoulder seams.

2. Front and neck band: With RS facing, #4 circular needle, and charcoal, pick up a total of 257 (279, 305, 331) sts:
    - Pick up 52 (58, 64, 70) sts from lower left front to first V-neck dec.
    - Pick up 58 (62, 68, 74) sts from V-neck dec to shoulder seam.
    - Pick up 37 (39, 41, 43) sts from shoulder to shoulder.
    - Pick up 58 (62, 68, 74) sts from shoulder seam to V-neck dec.
    - Pick up 52 (58, 64, 70) sts from V-neck dec to lower right front.
    - Work 6 more rows in K1, P1 rib with charcoal, then switch to black for 1 more row and BO. Place 5 (5, 6, 6) 2-stitch buttonholes, evenly spaced, between bottom front and first V-neck dec in 4th row of rib.

3. Armhole bands: With RS facing, #4 needles, and charcoal, pick up 120 (126, 138, 150) sts in K1, P1 rib.
    - Work 6 rows in charcoal, then switch to black for 1 more row plus the BO row.

4. Sew side seams.

5. Complete pockets:
    - With RS facing and #4 needles, work sts off of stitch holder onto needle, inc 1 st (M1) at beg and end of row in K1, P1 rib pattern [25 (25, 29, 29) sts].
    - Work 6 more rows in charcoal, then switch to black for 1 more row and the BO row.
    - Slipstitch pocket linings and edges of rib in place.

6. Block vest to desired measurements.

7. Stabilize back neck.

TIP

Select lightweight buttons for cardigans, particularly if the vest is going to be worn unbuttoned. This will reduce the risk of one side of the vest "growing" longer than the other with the weight of the buttons. You may also want to stabilize the button side of the front bands slightly. Refer to "Stabilizing Back Neck and Shoulders" on page 136, working one row of chain stitch along the pickup row from the wrong side.

THE FAMILY OF MAN

"The family is one of nature's masterpieces." —GEORGE SANTAYANA

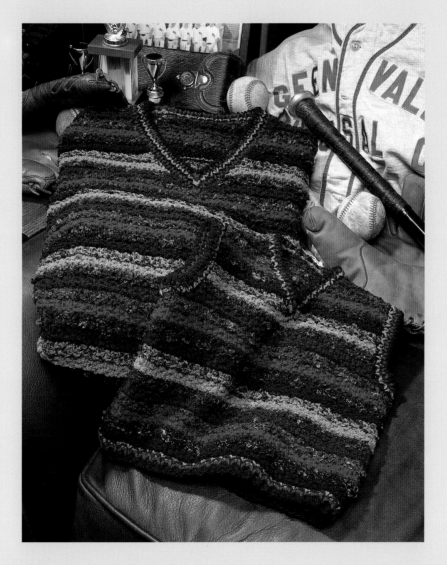

Many of us have childhood memories of favorite sweaters passed down through the family from older brothers, sisters, or cousins. These were our wearable history, passed from one child to the next until the cuffs were worn through. For some, the holiday family photos in coordinated outfits evoke fond memories. The emotional bond always seems as clear to us as the physical similarity between fathers and sons or grandsons who appear in matching sweaters, knit with such obvious care by those who know them best.

NONO JOE'S VEST

Nono is the Italian word for "Grandpa," and these two vests are a tribute to our second family, specifically "The Patriarch," Joe, and his grandson Joey! While neither of us was born with more than a trace of Italian ancestry, we have been truly fortunate to have been embraced by this wonderful, loving, spirited family. Our book wouldn't be complete without these sweaters—our tokens of thanks for the loan of their beautiful beach house for brainstorming and writing this book, for the incredible feasts we have enjoyed in the process, for the beauty of their gardens to inspire us, and most of all, for the love and encouragement of Elisabetta and her amazing family! We are honored to be, although not a part of the "original family," included in their extended family. We hope these vests will fit several generations!

SIZES

Small (Medium, Large, X-Large)
Finished Chest: 42 (46, 50, 54)"
Finished Length: 24 (25, 26, 27)"

MATERIALS

Use a yarn that knits at 3.65 sts to 1" in St st.
8 (8, 12, 12) total skeins of S. Charles
    Collezione Campo, 67% wool and 33%
    nylon, each approximately 88 yds [704
    (704, 1056, 1056) yds total], in the follow-
    ing colors:
        2 (2, 3, 3) skeins of navy #2
        2 (2, 3, 3) skeins of red #3
        2 (2, 3, 3) skeins of purple #5
        2 (2, 3, 3) skeins of sage #1
8 (8, 12, 12) total skeins of S. Charles
    Collezione Corso, 55% wool, 24% acrylic,
    and 21% nylon, each approximately 88 yds
    [704 (704, 1056, 1056) yds total], in the
    following colors:
        2 (2, 3, 3) skeins of navy #52
        2 (2, 3, 3) skeins of red #53
        2 (2, 3, 3) skeins of purple #55
        2 (2, 3, 3) skeins of sage #51

Note: The total number of yards for this pattern is 1408 (1408, 2112, 2112); there will be
a fair amount of leftover yarn with a pattern
like this.

#9 and #10 needles
Safety pin

GAUGE

15 sts and 26 rows = 4" in Hurdle stitch on
    #10 needles
Always check gauge before starting sweater.
    Increase or decrease needle size to obtain
    correct gauge.

"HURDLE" PATTERN STITCH

Row 1 (RS): Knit (garter st).
Row 2: Knit (garter st).
Row 3: *K1, P1*; rep from * to * (seed st).
Row 4: *K1, P1*; rep from * to * (seed st).
Rep rows 1–4.

COLOR SEQUENCE

Work 1 complete stitch pattern (4 rows) in
    each color (32-row repeat):

A	Campo	Navy
B	Corso	Navy
C	Campo	Red
D	Corso	Red
E	Campo	Purple
F	Corso	Purple
G	Campo	Sage
H	Corso	Sage

Repeat.

BACK

1. With #9 needles and color A, CO 75
    (81, 89, 97) sts. Work 8 rows in K1,

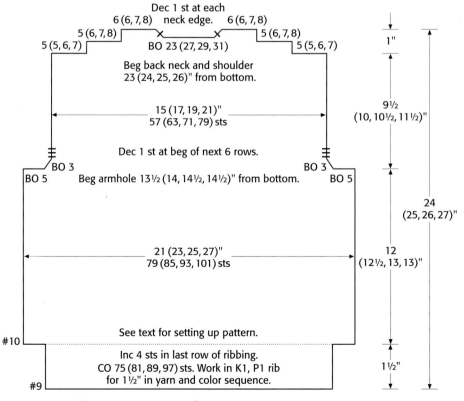

Dec 1 st at each
6 (6, 7, 8)   neck edge.   6 (6, 7, 8)
5 (6, 7, 8)   5 (6, 7, 8)
5 (5, 6, 7)   BO 23 (27, 29, 31)   5 (5, 6, 7)
Beg back neck and shoulder
23 (24, 25, 26)" from bottom.

15 (17, 19, 21)"
57 (63, 71, 79) sts

Dec 1 st at beg of next 6 rows.

BO 3   BO 3
BO 5   Beg armhole 13½ (14, 14½, 14½)" from bottom.   BO 5

21 (23, 25, 27)"
79 (85, 93, 101) sts

See text for setting up pattern.

#10

Inc 4 sts in last row of ribbing.
CO 75 (81, 89, 97) sts. Work in K1, P1 rib
for 1½" in yarn and color sequence.

#9

1"

9½
(10, 10½, 11½)"

24
(25, 26, 27)"

12
(12½, 13, 13)"

1½"

Back

P1 rib, changing colors every row in the following sequence: A, C, E, G. Rep this sequence 1 more time, inc 4 sts evenly in last row of rib. End with a WS row [79 (85, 93, 101) sts].

2. Switch to #10 needles and beg "Hurdle" pattern stitch, following color sequence. Cont until work measures 13½ (14, 14½, 14½)" from bottom [21 (23, 25, 27)" wide].

3. Beg armhole shaping:
   ◆ BO 5 sts at beg of next 2 rows.
   ◆ BO 3 sts at beg of next 2 rows.
   ◆ Dec 1 st at beg of next 6 rows. [57 (63, 71, 79) sts; 15 (17, 19, 21)" wide].

4. Cont until work measures 23 (24, 25, 26)" from bottom.

5. Beg back neck and shoulder shaping:
   ◆ BO first 5 (5, 6, 7) sts. Work next 11 (12, 14, 17) sts. Keeping 12 (13, 15, 17) sts on right-hand needle, BO center 23 (27, 29, 31) sts. Finish row. Turn work.
   ◆ BO first 5 (5, 6, 7) sts. Finish row to neck edge. Turn work.
   ◆ Dec 1 st at neck edge. Finish row. Turn work.
   ◆ BO 5 (6, 7, 8) sts. Finish row. Turn work.
   ◆ Work across row. Turn work.
   ◆ BO last 6 (6, 7, 8) sts.

6. Complete back neck and shoulder shaping:
   ◆ Join yarn at neck edge. Dec 1 st and finish row. Turn work.

◆ BO 5 (6, 7, 8) sts. Finish row. Turn work.
◆ Work across row. Turn work.
◆ BO last 6 (6, 7, 8) sts.

FRONT

1. Work front exactly the same as back until work measures 15 (16, 17, 18)" from bottom.

2. Beg V-neck shaping while completing armhole decreases:
   ◆ Work halfway across row, place center st on a safety pin, and finish row. Turn work.
   ◆ Complete right side of neck shap-

ing by dec 1 st at neck edge every 3 (3, 2, 2) rows 12 (14, 15, 16) times.
   ◆ Cont until work measures 23 (24, 25, 26)" from bottom.

3. Complete shoulder shaping:
   ◆ BO 5 (5, 6, 7) sts at outside edge. Finish row. Turn work.
   ◆ Work across row. Turn work.
   ◆ BO 5 (6, 7, 8) sts. Finish row. Turn work.
   ◆ Work across row.
   ◆ BO last 6 (6, 7, 8) sts.

4. Join yarn at neck edge, leaving center st on a pin. Complete left side the same as right side, but reverse shaping.

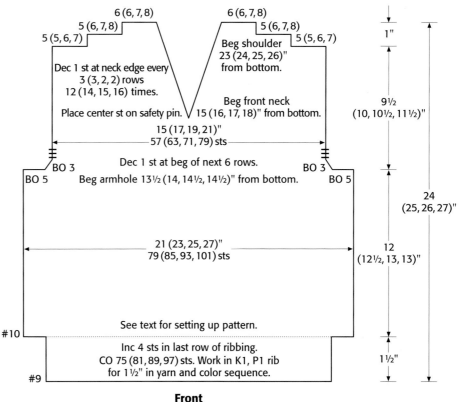

Front

FINISHING

1. Sew shoulders seams.

2. With RS facing, #9 needles, and color E, pick up a total of 94 (98, 100, 102) sts:

   ◆ Pick up 25 (29, 31, 33) sts across back neck from shoulder to shoulder.

   ◆ Pick up 34 sts from left shoulder to front center.

   ◆ Pick up center st, leaving it marked.

   ◆ Pick up 34 sts back to right shoulder.

   ◆ Work in K1, P1 rib, following the same rib sequence as bottom of sweater (work through sequence only once).

   ◆ To complete V-neck rib with single st at V, work to last st before center (marked) st and sl that st as if to purl.

   ◆ Put center st on a holder (to front of work) and knit slipped st and st to left of center together as one.

   ◆ Sl this st temporarily to right-hand needle so you can sl center (marked) st back onto right-hand needle.

   ◆ PSSO center (marked) st over st on right-hand needle. (Rep this dec every other time you come to the V.)

   ◆ Work in rib pattern for 1" and BO loosely. (Chinese BO is optional; see page 137.)

3. With RS facing, #9 needles, and color E, pick up 114 (118, 122, 130) sts for each armhole.

   ◆ Work in K1, P1 rib, following same sequence as neck for 1" and BO.

4. Sew side seams.

5. Block vest to desired measurements.

6. Stabilize back neck and shoulders.

> ### TIP
>
> Weave in ends as you knit (see "Some Knitting Basics" beginning on page 129) to avoid the overwhelming task of burying them all once the vest is completed.

LITTLE JOEY'S VEST

SIZES

Toddler: Small (Medium, Large)

Finished Chest: 22 (24, 26, 27)"

Finished Length: 11 (12, 13, 14)"

MATERIALS

Use a yarn that knits at 3.65 sts to 1".

4 skeins total of S. Charles Collezione Campo, each approximately 88 yds [352 yds total], in the following colors:

    1 skein of navy #2

    1 skein of red #3

    1 skein of purple #5

    1 skein of sage #1

4 skeins total of S. Charles Collezione Corso, each approximately 88 yds [352 yds total], in the following colors:

    1 skein of navy #52

    1 skein of red #53

    1 skein of purple #55

    1 skein of sage #51

Note: The total number of yards for this pattern is 704; there will be a fair amount of left-over yarn with a pattern like this.

#9 and #10 needles

Safety pin

GAUGE

15 sts and 26 rows = 4" in Hurdle stitch on #10 needles

Always check gauge before starting sweater. Increase or decrease needle size to obtain correct gauge.

"HURDLE" PATTERN STITCH

Row 1 (RS): Knit (garter st).

Row 2: Knit (garter st).

Row 3: *K1, P1*; rep from * to * (seed st).

Row 4: *K1, P1*; rep from * to * (seed st).

Rep rows 1–4.

COLOR SEQUENCE

Work 1 complete stitch pattern (4 rows) in each color (32-row repeat):

A	Campo	Navy
B	Corso	Navy
C	Campo	Red
D	Corso	Red
E	Campo	Purple
F	Corso	Purple
G	Campo	Sage
H	Corso	Sage

Repeat.

BACK

1. With #9 needles and color A, CO 43 (47, 51, 55) sts. Work 8 rows in K1, P1 rib, changing colors every row in the following sequence: A, C, E, G. End with WS row.

2. Switch to #10 needles and beg "Hurdle" pattern stitch, following color sequence. Cont until work measures 6½ (7, 8, 8½)" from bottom [11 (12, 13, 14)" wide].

3. Beg armhole shaping:
   ◆ BO 4 sts at beg of next 2 rows.
   ◆ BO 2 sts at beg of next 2 rows.

◆ Dec 1 st at beg of next 2 rows [29 (33, 35, 39) sts; 7 (8, 9, 10)" wide].

4. Cont until work measures 10½ (11½, 12½, 13½)" from bottom.

5. Beg back neck and shoulder shaping:
   ◆ Work across first 6 (8, 8, 10) sts. BO center 17 (17, 19, 19) sts and finish row. Turn work.
   ◆ Work back to neck edge. Turn work.
   ◆ Dec 1 st at neck edge. Finish row. Turn work.
   ◆ BO last 5 (7, 7, 9) sts.

6. Complete back neck and shoulder shaping:
   ◆ Join yarn at neck edge. Dec 1 st and finish row. Turn work.
   ◆ BO last 5 (7, 7, 9) sts.

FRONT

1. Work front exactly the same as back until work measures 7 (8, 9, 10)" from bottom.

2. Beg V-neck shaping while completing armhole shaping:
   ◆ Work halfway across row, place center st on a safety pin, and finish row. Turn work.
   ◆ Complete right side of neck shaping by dec 1 st at neck edge EOR 9 (9, 10, 10) times.
   ◆ Cont until work measures 11 (12, 13, 14)" from bottom.
   ◆ BO 5 (7, 7, 9) sts straight across.

3. Join yarn at neck edge, leaving center st marked. Complete left side the same as right side, but reverse shaping.

FINISHING

1. Sew shoulder seams.

2. With RS facing, #9 needles, and color E, pick up a total of 60 (60, 62, 62) sts:
   ◆ Pick up 19 (19, 21, 21) sts across back neck from shoulder to shoulder.
   ◆ Pick up 20 sts from left shoulder to front center.

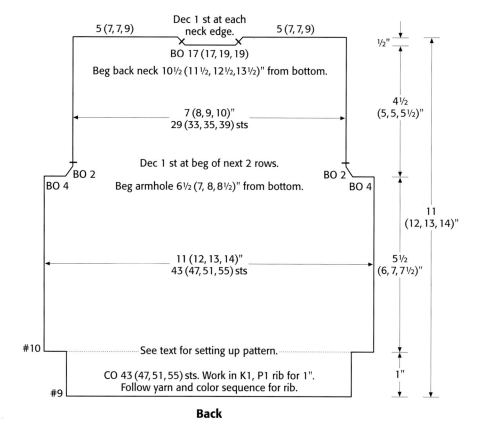

Back

- Pick up center st, leaving it marked.
- Pick up 20 sts back to right shoulder.
- Work in K1, P1 rib, following same rib sequence as bottom of sweater (work through sequence only once).
- To complete V-neck rib with single st at V, work to last st before center (marked) st and sl that st as if to purl.
- Put center st on a holder (to front of work) and knit slipped st and st to left of center together as one.

- Sl this st temporarily to right-hand needle so you can sl center (marked) st back onto right-hand needle.
- PSSO center (marked) st over st on right-hand needle. (Rep this dec every other time you come to V.)
- Work in rib pattern for 1" and BO loosely. (Chinese BO is optional; see page 137.)

3. With RS facing, #9 needles, and color E, pick up 46 (50, 54, 54) sts for each armhole.

4. Working in K1, P1 rib and following same sequence as neck, cont for 1" and BO.

5. Sew side seams.

6. Block vest to desired measurements.

7. Stabilize back neck and shoulders.

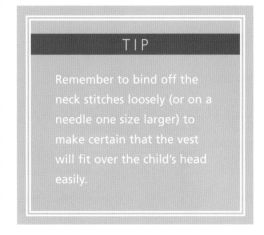

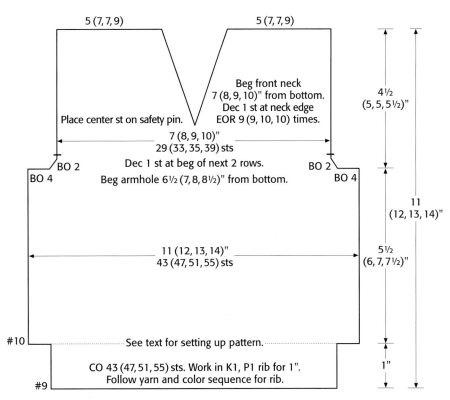

5 (7, 7, 9)   5 (7, 7, 9)

Beg front neck
7 (8, 9, 10)" from bottom.
Dec 1 st at neck edge
EOR 9 (9, 10, 10) times.

Place center st on safety pin.

7 (8, 9, 10)"
29 (33, 35, 39) sts

Dec 1 st at beg of next 2 rows.
Beg armhole 6½ (7, 8, 8½)" from bottom.

BO 2   BO 2
BO 4   BO 4

4½
(5, 5, 5½)"

11
(12, 13, 14)"

11 (12, 13, 14)"
43 (47, 51, 55) sts

5½
(6, 7, 7½)"

#10

See text for setting up pattern.

CO 43 (47, 51, 55) sts. Work in K1, P1 rib for 1".
Follow yarn and color sequence for rib.

1"

#9

Front

SOME KNITTING BASICS

Here is our list of knitting basics that can never be repeated too many times.

Casting On

Cast on to a needle one size larger than the one specified, then change to the specified needle size on your first row. This ensures that your cast-on row is not too tight.

Knitting Your Edge Stitches

We always knit the first and last stitch of every row (including purl and pattern rows). This creates a clean, uniform "selvage edge" for weaving pieces together when the garment is complete.

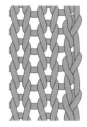

Selvage edge of
stockinette stitch

Picking Up Dropped Stitches

It is not unusual to drop a stitch and for that stitch to ravel down one or more rows. Use a crochet hook to pick up the dropped stitches. Insert the hook, front to back, into the loop of the dropped stitch. Use the hook to catch the first horizontal "ladder" in the knitting and pull it through the loop to the front. Continue in this manner through all the ladders. Place the loop on the needle, making certain that the right side of the U is on the front of the needle.

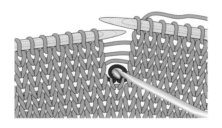

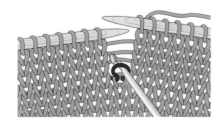

Picking up a dropped knit stitch

If you drop a stitch on a purl row, turn the work around and correct as described above for the knit side, making sure to turn the work back around to finish the purl row. Or, you can pick up the dropped stitch from behind by inserting the crochet hook, back to front, into the loop of the dropped stitch, placing the first horizontal ladder in front of the stitch and pulling the ladder through the loop to the back. Continue in this manner through all the ladders. Place the last loop on the needle, making sure the right side of the U is on the front of the needle.

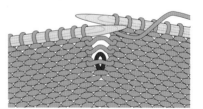

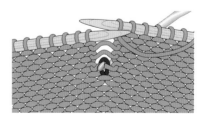

Picking up a dropped purl stitch

When an edge stitch drops and ravels, there will be no visible ladders to chain up with a crochet hook. Instead, you will see a large loop extending from the edge above a small loop, below which the knitted edge is intact. To correct this error, insert the crochet hook into the small loop. Holding the large loop with some tension, pull the lower portion of the large loop through the loop on the hook to form a stitch; then pull the upper part of the large loop through the loop on the hook to form a stitch. Finally, catch the working yarn and pull it through the loop on the hook. Place the last stitch on the needle.

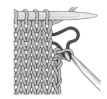

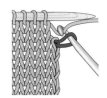

Picking up a dropped edge stitch

Joining Yarns

There are several methods of joining yarns when starting a new skein or changing colors. We like to knit both the old and new yarn into the first stitch when beginning a row, and then, dropping the old yarn, continue across the row. Remember, when you work back across the row, that first stitch is just one stitch, even though you have two strands in the stitch.

Start a new skein of yarn at the beginning of a row whenever possible. When changing in the middle of a row cannot be avoided, *do not* knot the yarn. Leave a generous 3" tail from both the old and new skeins and continue knitting. These ends can be woven in securely and invisibly; knotting your yarns will leave a "scar" in your work.

Weaving in Ends As You Knit

To avoid hours of laborious darning after your sweater is complete (particularly on sweaters where you change yarns frequently or in two-color work), you should get into the practice of weaving in the ends as you go.

It is important that the weaving is done at a relaxed, even tension, or the knitting will pucker. To do this, leave ends approximately 3" on the old and new yarns; work the next two stitches with the new yarn, then, holding both yarns in your left hand, lay them over the working yarn and work the next stitch. Continue in this way, laying the ends over the working yarn on every other stitch and knitting past the ends on the following stitch for at least 2".

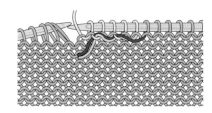

Increasing Your Stitches

There is more than one way to increase the number of stitches on your needle. You can make two stitches out of one by knitting into the front and back of the same stitch. This may also be done purlwise by purling into the front and back of the same stitch, or it may be worked by knit 1, purl 1 into one stitch, or by purl 1, knit 1 into one stitch.

Another method, called "Make One (M1)," adds a new stitch without leaving a hole. Insert the left-hand needle from front to back into the horizontal strand between the last stitch worked and the next stitch on the left-hand needle. Knit this strand through the back loop to twist the stitch.

Decreasing Your Stitches

There are also several ways to decrease the number of stitches on your needle. With the yarn in back, slip one stitch, knit one stitch, and pass the slipped stitch over; that is, insert the point of the left-hand needle into the slipped stitch and draw it over the knit stitch and off the right-hand needle.

You can also slip the first and second stitches knitwise, one at a time, then insert the tip of the left-hand needle into the fronts of these two stitches from the left, and knit them together from this position. This is known as slip, slip, knit.

For V-neck ribbing with one center stitch, slip two as to knit, knit one; pass the slipped stitch over. For V-neck ribbing with two center stitches, knit two together and then slip, slip, knit.

Knitting Basic Cables

For a front cross, leave the cable needle holding the stitches in front of the work while working the other stitches behind it.

For a back cross, leave the cable needle holding the stitches in back of the work while working the other stitches in front.

For a twisted rib, knit the second stitch first in back of the work without taking it off the needle, then knit the first stitch as usual. Take both stitches off the left-hand needle.

Binding Off

Binding off secures the last row of knitting so that it will not ravel. Binding off is also used for shaping when two or more stitches need to be eliminated at one time, such as at armholes and necklines.

Always bind off in pattern. Many knitters tend to bind off too tightly, causing puckers and undue stress on the bound-off edge. You can prevent this problem by binding off with a knitting needle one or two sizes larger than the one called for in the pattern.

To bind off on a knit row, first knit two stitches, then *with the two stitches on the right-hand needle, pass the right stitch over the left and off the end of the needle. Knit the next stitch.* Repeat from * to * until the required number of stitches are bound off.

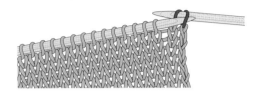

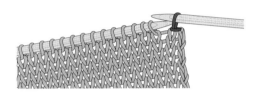

The process is the same for binding off on the purl side, except that you'll purl instead of knit. For ribbing, or for any other pattern stitch, bind off in the pattern; that is, knit the knit stitches and purl the purl stitches, always passing the right stitch over the left and off the end of the needle. After binding off all the stitches on the needle, cut the working yarn and pull the cut end through the last stitch to secure it.

Finishing is what separates the hand-made sweater from the merely homemade. We have included specific methods that we find work best for the sweaters in this book. When you have finished all the pieces of your garment, lay them out and measure them against the pattern for each piece again. It is much easier to make any corrections or alterations at this point, rather than waiting until the garment is sewn together. Pin the pieces together and try the garment on before burying the ends or sewing the pieces together.

Sewing Shoulder Seams

This method seams the shoulders by pulling the seaming yarn tight enough to cover the bound-off edges. The finished seam resembles a knit row and requires the same number of stitches on each bound-off edge.

Working from the right side with the bound-off edges lined up stitch for stitch, begin by inserting a threaded tapestry needle from back to front into the V of the stitch just below the bound-off edge.

Insert the needle under two strands of the knit stitch on the opposite piece, then under the next two strands of the first piece. Adjust the tension so that the seam looks like the knitted work; repeat from * to * to the end of the bound-off edge.

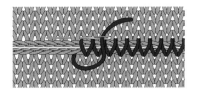

Sewing Side Seams

Work this seam from the right side of the knitting, placing the pieces to be seamed on a table, right side up. Begin at the lower edge and work upward, row by row. Insert a threaded tapestry needle under two horizontal bars between the first and second stitches from the edge on one side of the seam, then under two corresponding bars on the opposite side. Continue taking stitches alternately from side to side. Pull the yarn in the direction of the seam, not toward your body, to

prevent the bars from stretching to the front.

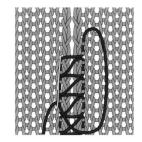

Picking Up Stitches to Knit Bands

Stitches are picked up to create finished neckbands, cardigan borders, and collars. Always pick up stitches from the right side, using a separate skein of yarn and a needle one or two sizes smaller than you used to knit the body of the garment.

Many patterns will tell you to "pick up and knit" a specific number of stitches. Read literally, this is somewhat misleading—you should not pick up a stitch and knit it. You should pick up a stitch as if to knit, then leave it on the needle. When all the stitches are on the needle, turn the work and begin your pattern in the next row.

For neckbands, begin at the right corner of the edge where you are picking up stitches. Insert the needle under two strands of the selvage-edge stitch, wrap the needle as if to knit, pull the loop through to the right side, and leave the newly made stitch on the needle. Continue working from right to left.

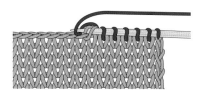

Picked-up stitches can cause holes to form in the garment, especially along curved edges. Watch for these and, if you see one, take out that stitch and pick it up elsewhere. Continue until the desired number of stitches are on the needle.

When picking up stitches along the vertical front edge of a cardigan, you will be picking up from the side, not the top of the stitch. The formula for picking up the correct number of evenly spaced stitches is as follows: Your edge stitches form a series of small "bumps" or points along the selvage edge. Beginning at the right side of the work, insert the needle into the hole under the first bump. Now insert your needle into the hole underneath the bar between the first two bumps; repeat in the bar between the second and third bumps. Pick up the fourth stitch in the hole behind the third bump.

Repeat this process (bar, bar, bump) along the length of the front band.

To make sure the picked-up stitches are evenly spaced, divide the knitted edge into fourths (or eighths for a very long edge) and mark these divisions with open stitch markers. Pick up one-fourth (or one-eighth) of the desired total number of stitches in each section.

Setting In Sleeve Caps

With the right side of the pieces facing you, fold the sleeve in half lengthwise to find the center. Pin the center point of the cap to the outer edge of the shoulder seam, then pin the beginning point of the sleeve-cap shaping to the lowest point of the armhole, both front and back. Now ease the cap into the armhole evenly and pin in place. Sew in the sleeve as you would a side seam, taking care not to pull the working yarn too tight; you want to avoid distorting the armhole.

Note that we do some cap shaping even with drop shoulder patterns; this

eliminates the bulk of extra fabric under the arms when the sweater is sewn together. To set in a drop shoulder where there is no armhole shaping on the body of the sweater, measure from the shoulder seam to the desired armhole depth and place pins in both front and back to identify sleeve placement.

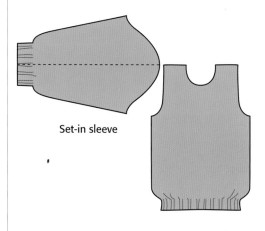

Set-in sleeve

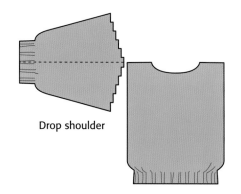

Drop shoulder

Making Buttonholes

A visible horizontal buttonhole is neat, firm, and requires no reinforcing. The lower edge of the buttonhole is worked from the right side of the garment; the upper edge is worked from the wrong side.

To work a one-row buttonhole:

1. Work to the position where you want the buttonhole, bring the yarn to the front, slip the next stitch purlwise, and then return the yarn to the back.

2. *Slip the next stitch; then on the right-hand needle, pass the second stitch over the end stitch and drop it off the needle.* Repeat from * to * 3 times. Slip the last bound-off stitch to the left needle and turn the work.

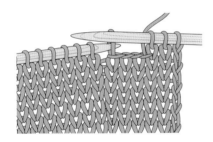

3. Move the yarn to the back and use the cable cast-on to cast on 5 stitches as follows: *Insert the right needle between the first and second stitches on the left needle, draw up a loop,

and place it on the left needle.* Repeat from * to * 4 times. Turn the work.

4. With the yarn in back, slip the first stitch from the left needle and pass the extra cast-on stitch over it to close the buttonhole. Work to the end of the row.

To correctly space buttonholes, one buttonhole needs to be within a couple of stitches from the top of the band, and one a couple of stitches from the bottom. The balance of the buttonholes should be evenly spaced between the top and bottom buttonholes.

Select your buttons before knitting the buttonholes rather than trying to find a button that fits the hole.

Making Crocheted Edges

Crocheted edges are usually narrower than knitted borders and provide a simple, clean edge. Single crochet and reverse crochet (also called shrimp or crab stitch) are the most popular crocheted edges for knitted garments. Single crochet makes a smooth finish; crab stitch makes a decorative beadlike finish.

SINGLE CROCHET

Working from right to left, insert the crochet hook into the knit edge stitch, draw up a loop, bring the yarn over the hook, and draw this loop through the first one. *Insert the hook into the next stitch, draw up the loop, bring the yarn over the hook again, and draw this loop through both loops on the hook*; repeat from * to * until the entire edge has been covered. Cut the yarn and secure the last loop by pulling the tail through it.

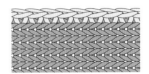

REVERSE CROCHET
(shrimp or crab stitch)

We always work one row of single crochet first, then follow with a row of crab stitch. Working from left to right, insert the crochet hook into a single crochet stitch, draw up a loop, bring the yarn over the hook, and draw this loop through the first one. *Insert the hook into the next stitch to the right, draw up a loop, bring the yarn over the hook again, and draw this loop through both loops on the hook*; repeat from * to * until the entire edge has been covered. Cut the yarn and secure the last loop by pulling the tail through it.

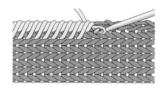

Stabilizing Back Neck and Shoulders

We stabilize all our sweaters to anchor the seams and to keep them from growing or stretching across the shoulders, causing them to appear sloppy or ill-fitting.

Work one row of chain stitch on the inside shoulder seam of the sweater from one shoulder across the back neck to the opposite shoulder. If necessary, pull in slightly by increasing the tension as you work to narrow the shoulders and neck up to an inch on each side as needed for proper fit.

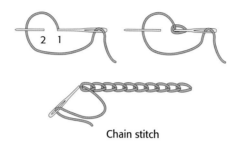

Chain stitch

Blocking

Blocking is the process of dampening or steaming the knitted pieces to even out the lines of the stitches and the yarn fibers. The labels on most knitting fibers give instructions for blocking. Read the instructions before you begin.

Blocking requires a large, flat surface. Block on an out-of-the-way place on the carpet or make a special padded steaming table for this purpose. Use long straight pins, such as quilting or stainless T-pins, to pin the garment to the blocking surface. First pin the length, then the width, and finally the curves and/or corners, measuring carefully at every step to ensure that it matches the dimensions given in the pattern. Place pins every 1" to prevent the piece from shrinking as it dries. If you block on a very large surface, such as a carpet, you can pin the pieces next to each other, lining up the selvage edges that will be steamed to make sure the seams are even.

Hold a steamer or iron set on the steam setting ½" above the knitted surface and direct the steam over the entire surface, except the ribbing. There are several good hand steamers on the market today in the $40 to $50 range. You can get similar results by placing wet cheesecloth on top of the knitted surface and touching it lightly with a dry iron. Do not press down or use a forward or sideways motion.

Never steam-block ribbing that you want to remain elastic, such as in the waist and cuff area. Once blocked, ribbing will remain stretched out. However, you should block ribbing along a front cardigan border to flatten it and prevent it from pulling.

Press the seams of your garment as they are sewn. Take care not to mash the yarn in the seam area, but do dampen the seam on the inside of the garment, using steam or a spray bottle (according to yarn type) and gently finger-press the seam to reduce the bulk.

Hand-knit garments can be machine washed on the gentle cycle in your washing machine in a sweater (net) bag. Refer to the care instructions on the yarn label. Washing with very mild soap (we recommend Forever New) and drying flat on a drying rack will ensure long life. Remove as much water as possible by pressing it between dry towels before laying it flat to dry. Make sure the water temperature on both wash and rinse cycles is cool.

Chinese Bind Off

This is a bind-off method taught to us by Yiming Zhi, who came to Tricoter soon after she moved to Seattle from China; that's why we have called it the Chinese Bind Off. We have never seen it described in a book, although Yiming assures us that it is a very common technique in her native China. You will find that it is more time-consuming than our traditional bind off, but the extra time is well worth the beautiful finished edge that it creates. Our good friend and talented knitter Blaise Wren, a relatively new knitter and technical writer by trade, was intrigued by the beauty and complexity of this bind off and volunteered to write the directions below.

Step-by-step instructions follow, but what you are doing with this bind off is knitting all purl stitches and purling all knit stitches, binding off each stitch as it is formed. The stitch on the right needle is temporarily transferred to the left needle. The yarn is then moved, and the transferred stitch is returned to the right needle. The next stitch is then formed. If this sounds a bit confusing, these directions may help to clarify things.

1. Work (knit) the edge stitch.
2. Purl the first (knit) stitch.
3. Bind off the first stitch on the right needle (insert the left needle into the first stitch on the right needle, then pull it over the second stitch and off the right needle).
4. Transfer the remaining stitch on the right needle to the left needle.
5. Move yarn to back of work, then return the transferred stitch on the left needle to the right needle.
6. Knit the next (purl) stitch. There should now be two stitches on your right needle.
7. Bind off the first stitch on the right needle.
8. Transfer the remaining stitch on the right needle to the left needle.
9. Move yarn to front of work.
10. Return the transferred stitch on the left needle to the right needle.
11. Purl the next (knit) stitch. There should now be two stitches on the right needle.
12. Repeat steps 3–11.

Tassels

Supplies
- Combination of coordinating yarns (no specific gauge or type)
- Cardboard
- Scissors
- Tapestry needle

DIRECTIONS

1. Cut cardboard 1" longer than the finished length of the tassel. Place all yarns in a basket, shopping bag, or box. Take 1 strand of each yarn and wrap them all together as one around the cardboard square. Count the number of wraps as you go. (In the event that you want to duplicate the tassel, you will need to know this.) Wrap your yarns at least 25 to 35 times—you want a fat tassel! Cut the

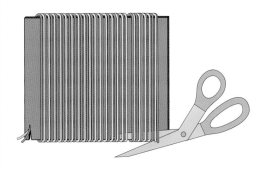

wrapped yarns along the bottom of the cardboard square and place the lengths of yarn flat on a table.

2. Make a twisted cord about 20" long (see below). Place the cord flat on the table; take your cut yarns and place them on top of the cord. Tie the ends of the cord firmly around the yarn once, check to see that the yarns are "centered" on the cord, then tie the cord tightly one more time to secure the tassel.

3. Fold the cut yarns in half with the twisted cord at the top and wrap the "neck" of the tassel with one strand of the yarn that you have used in your tassel. Hold this strand along the side of the tassel and, starting at the top of the neck, wrap the yarn evenly and tightly around the neck. This secures the tail and becomes a part of the tassel. Thread a tapestry needle with the opposite end of the yarn and go back and forth through the neck of the tassel several more times. To secure

this end, go one half of the way through the neck of the tassel and then down through the center of the tassel toward the bottom.

4. Hold the tassel in your left hand and cut the strands of yarn evenly across the bottom.

5. Holding it with tongs, steam the tassel over a teakettle. This will smooth and fluff the tassel. Use a crochet hook to tie the ends to your pillow or throw.

Twisted Cord

Supplies
- Hand drill with a cup hook in the bit
- Cup hooks
- Fishing weight with a curtain hook in the loop
- Coordinating yarns used in (or complementary to) throw or muffler

DIRECTIONS

1. Select your yarns and decide on the desired length of your finished cord. Multiply the finished length by 4 to get the correct length of the fibers. You may combine several strands of your fibers (these can be all the same or coordinating fibers). The thickness of the finished cord will depend on the number and type of fibers chosen and the end use of the twisted cord itself. Experiment to find the thickness you desire.

2. Holding combined fibers together as one, tie a knot in each end of the combined fibers.

3. Place a cup hook in a doorjamb or doorframe at approximately waist height from the floor.

4. Loop one end of your fibers over the hook on the door and the other end in the hook already in the drill. Holding the drill, stand far enough from the door to maintain tension in the fibers.

5. Twist the fibers by winding the drill, counting the number of times you wind as you go. (You will need this information if you decide to duplicate the twisted cord.) Some combinations of fibers require more winding than others.

6. When the cord draws you toward the doorframe as it shortens (due to the twisting), it is almost ready for

the next step. To check the tension, take hold of the twisted cord 6" from the drill, maintaining firm tension between the doorframe and your hand. Let the tension "relax" slightly between your hand and the drill; the cord should twist into tight knots if the cord has been twisted enough at this point. If more winding is needed, remember to keep track of the number of winds.

7. Holding the drill in your left hand, take the weight in your right hand and place it in the center of the twisted cord. Keeping the cord taut, place both ends of the cord on the cup hook attached to the drill. Hold the drill up so that the weight twists freely. When it has stopped spinning, remove the weight, take the two ends off of the cup hook in the drill bit, and knot the ends together to secure the twisted cord.

8. To finish the cord, put one end back on the doorframe hook and the other on the drill hook. Reverse-twist the drill 20 times. Take the cord off of the drill hook and let it unwind. This takes the bias out of the cord.

BARBER POLE TWISTED CORD
(Two Colors)

Cut each color fiber one-half the finished length of the cord. Loop one color through the other to create two U's hooked together. Knot each end and wind on the drill as outlined above. When folded in half, this cord looks like a barber pole.

TRICOTER SPECIAL SERVICES

It is our commitment at Tricoter to offer the most luxurious, unique fibers and ornamentation available in the European and domestic markets and to assist you in the design and creation of your own one-of-a-kind, hand-knit garment or home accessory. Tricoter offers complimentary design services and guidance through the completion of projects to all of our customers. We believe that it is the detail and finishing that elevates a garment from "loving-hands-at-home" to a beautiful hand-knit original. Therefore, we offer a variety of classes from basic skills through advanced techniques and finishing.

Because we realize your time is precious, Tricoter is also pleased to offer a variety of custom knitting and finishing services for those occasions when you require professional assistance. We have a number of out-of-town customers with whom we work on a regular basis to assist in the completion of hand-knit garments. The following is a brief outline of our services:

- Expert finishing services are available at an hourly rate. You can turn your work-in-progress over to us at any stage.

◆ We offer a variety of custom knitting services for your convenience. All garments are individually fitted and beautifully finished. We will work with you to design and create a sweater, jacket, coat, or garment of your choice that reflects your individual style.

◆ We have one of the most extensive collections of the finest hand-painted needlepoint canvases, fibers, and accessories available in the Pacific Northwest. We offer both individual and small-class instruction for needlework, and professional blocking and finishing for all of your needlepoint projects.

We have an appreciation for beautiful fibers and fine design, and we share our expertise and assistance with you—from the selection of fibers to a design that reflects your individual style. Please feel free to contact us for additional information regarding any of these services.

Tricoter
3121 E. Madison Street
Seattle, WA 98112
Phone: (206) 328-6505
Fax: (206) 328-0635
Toll Free: 1-877-554-YARN
1-877-554-9276
E-mail: tricoter@aol.com
Web Site: www.tricoter.com

Yarn Resources

For a list of shops in your area that carry the yarns and buttons mentioned in the book, call or write to the following companies.

Filatura di Crosa & S.Charles
Tahki • Stacy Charles
1059 Manhattan Avenue
Brooklyn, NY 11222
(800) 962-8002

Noro & On Line
Knitting Fever, Inc.
35 Debevoise Avenue
Roosevelt, NY 11575-0502
(800) 645-3457

Horstia
Muench Yarns & Buttons
285 Bel Marin Keys Boulevard, Unit J
Novato, CA 94949
(800) 733-8080

Lang
Berroco, Inc.
14 Elmdale Road
Uxbridge, MA 01569-0367
(800) 343-4948

Karabella
Karabella Yarns, Inc.
1201 Broadway
New York, NY 10001
(800) 550-0898

Aurora & Garn
Garnstudio/Drops Design
2385 Carlos Street
PO Box 3068
Moss Beach, CA 94038
(800) 637-3207

Baruffa
Lana Borgosesia NA, Inc.
527 S Tejon, Suite 200
Colorado Springs, CO 80903
(800) 431-1999

Great Adirondack
Great Adirondack Yarn Company
950 County Highway 126
Amsterdam, NY 10210
(518) 843-3381

Mission Falls
Unique Kolours, Ltd.
1428 Oak Lane
Downington, PA 19334
(800) 252-3934

Bibliography

Fassett, Kaffe. *Glorious Knits*. New York: Clarkson N. Potter, Inc., 1985.

Complete Guide to Needlepoint. Pleasantville, N.Y.: Reader's Digest Association, Inc., 1979.

Square, Vicki. *The Knitter's Companion*. Loveland, Colo.: Interweave Press, Inc., 1996. The best "carry-along" reference book we've found—small, sturdy, lightweight, and complete!

Vogue Knitting. New York: Pantheon Books, 1989. *The* comprehensive source to your hand-knitting questions in easy-to-understand language with clear, concise illustrations.